Dashboard Jesus

Distinctive Reminders

For Distracted Men

Clay Crosse

ISBN-13:
978-0615727806 (Holy Homes Books)

ISBN-10:
0615727808

Some of the anecdotal illustrations in this book are true to life and are included with the permission of the persons involved. All other illustrations are composites of real situations, and any resemblance to people living or dead is coincidental.

Unless otherwise identified, all Scripture quotations in this publication are taken from the *Holy Bible*, New Living Translation (NLT), copyright © 1996, 2004. Used by permission of Tyndale House Publishers, Inc., Wheaton, Illinois 60189. All rights reserved. Other versions used include: *THE MESSAGE* (MSG). Copyright © 1993, 1994, 1995, 1996, 2000, 2001, 2002. Used by permission of NavPress Publishing Group; the New King James Version (NKJV). Copyright © 1982 by Thomas Nelson, Inc. Used by permission. All rights reserved; the *Holy Bible, New International Version®* (NIV®). Copyright © 1973, 1978, 1984 by International Bible Society. Used by permission of Zondervan. All rights reserved; and the King James Version (KJV).

I dedicate this to every man who ever took the time, got involved, and placed reminders in my life that pointed me to a clearer focus on Christ.

CONTENTS

Foreword   7

Acknowledgments   11

Preface: A Message from Clay   13

Meet Dashboard Jesus   19

The Number-One Distraction   39

Uhh . . . I'm Not Much of a Reader   63

So . . . Who'd Like to Say Grace?   97

I'm Just a Workin' Man   123

Who, Me? Do That?   153

Jesus Calls Shotgun   183

Notes   203

About the author   207

Clay Crosse

Foreword

I remember sitting at Knott's Berry Farm in Buena Park, California, in 1994. It was New Year's Eve. I was there with my girlfriend, Jeanette, who is now my wife. We were both attending a college nearby, and on New Year's Eve a bunch of Christian artists always performed at Knott's. I remember watching Plankeye, the Supertones, and then, to slow it down a bit, we listened to a new artist named Clay Crosse. No band, no huge stage—just a guy with a powerful voice belting out some powerful songs.

Ten years later, I was ordering twelve cases of Jesus bobbleheads, twelve cases of Jesus air fresheners, and twenty-four cases of dashboard Jesuses (my personal favorite). I had started a ministry called XXXchurch.com to help those who were caught up with lust, porn, and other sexual issues find the freedom that can only come from knowing Christ. I had received a mail-order catalog that contained products you would find at Spencer Gifts, Urban Outfitters, and other novelty stores—only they were Christian themed. I was floored when I realized I could sell them on XXXchurch.com. It made sense to me. Especially the dashboard Jesus—simply a plastic figurine people could attach to the dashboard of their cars to remind them of the real Jesus.

I never imagined the backlash I would receive over the next several months! Needless to say, some people were not fans of the Jesus air freshener and the dashboard Jesus. They took it way too seriously. Jesus, who lived a perfect life and died a brutal death on the cross, was now moving back and forth on dashboards nationwide, and folks were incensed.

I listened to the complaints but looked at it in a much different way. For everyone who thought the dashboard Jesus was a joke (or worse), another person found the plastic Jesus meaningful. Including Clay Crosse.

I just finished reading Clay's book *Dashboard Jesus*. Yes, the book you are holding in your hand. Clay gets it, my friend. Men face distractions every day that threaten to lead them astray. For him, a plastic dashboard Jesus is part of a strategy to stay focused on what's important.

I travel the country speaking about pornography, but the issue of porn is not what I focus my talks on. Paul said in Romans 7:21 that "sin is there to trip me up" (MSG). Sin will keep you from doing what God wants you do to with your life. Whether they're on the computer, at work, in your mind, or on the television, these things take more and more of your time and become bigger and bigger distractions.

I remember hearing the news about Clay Crosse: His life, his marriage, and his music career all came to a sudden halt because of some bad choices Clay made in his life. He lost focus and became more and more distracted. Over the last seven years, I've heard stories like Clay's almost daily. I have seen men lose their jobs. I have seen marriages destroyed. I have personally taken people to jail. I receive letters from prisoners in jail on a weekly basis. So when I tell you that pornography is a serious problem for a lot of men, I'm not kidding.

Last week, I received a donation to our ministry in the mail. Along with the check was a photo of a husband and wife with their two daughters. The letter, written by the wife, simply said thank you. She had lost her husband to suicide a month before. He'd left a note explaining why he had to take his life: He was unfaithful. He told her she was his only true life, but throughout their marriage and during all the time he had spent on the road, he had made some poor choices. That was why he ended up taking his life.

This is serious stuff! This is not just some cute book with a trendy plastic Jesus figurine on the cover. I hope you get it. I hope you take this seriously. Clay will be the first person to tell you that he does not want you to head down the road he took. He talks openly about the distractions that all men face and gives you some solid advice to stay focused on the real Jesus. Enjoy!

—CRAIG GROSS, founder, XXXchurch.com

Clay Crosse

Acknowledgments

Special thanks to my amazing wife, Renee. You are precious to me, and I am so blessed to share this life with you! To our children Shelby, Savannah, Garrett, and Sophie, you are gifts to me, and I intend to keep you pointed to the Giver! I also want to thank Pastor Brian Carlisle and Faith Baptist Church, Arlington, Tennessee; Pastor Danny Sinquefield and Faith Baptist Church, Bartlett, Tennessee; Kris Wallen and NavPress; Jamie Chavez; Dennis and Kayla Fioravanti; Chris Beatty; Randall Gordon; America World Adoption Agency; Jim and Diana Hamilton; Brian and Gretchen Anderson; McPherson Guitars; Michael Henson; Linda Rosen; Tim and Cathy Hasenstab; Mel and Cassandra Senter; Dr. Gene and Peggy Brown; Gary McSpadden; LifeWay; Trinity Broadcasting; Craig Gross and XXXchurch; John and Irene Ng; Steve Gallagher; Tim Nicholson; Ken, Casey, Terri, Del, Jennifer, Chris, Mom and Dad; Scottie and Wilma; and to all our other financial and prayer partners here at HolyHomes Ministries. Thank you so much! We need you and are thankful God has placed you in our lives.

Clay Crosse

Preface: A Message from Clay

I will always *remind* you about these things—even though you already know them and are standing firm in the truth you have been taught. And it is only right that I should keep on *reminding* you as long as I live.

—2 Peter 1:12-13

Men need reminders. Over and over in life, we get distracted, we forget, and we just need to be reminded about things you'd think would be too important to forget.

Yet we do.

I wrote this book because I am one absentminded man. And I run into other forgetful men everywhere I go. Let's be honest here: Christian guys are slow to get it sometimes. Seriously, we can be just plain dumb! (And I honestly include myself in this.)

But it's not that we are dummies. God created us with

great intelligence and amazing potential. More accurately, it boils down to the reality that we get distracted. We are hardheaded. We are prideful. We are overly competitive. We are overworked. And we can be arrogant and self-centered. We also tend to get defeated. We get depressed. We freak out from time to time. And through it all, we are supposed to stay focused on God. *Hmmm . . .* not so easy, it seems.

Are you like me? You know the truth. You are 100 percent on board with what the Bible says, and you have complete security in that. You would never be talked out of your core beliefs for any amount of money. God is the truth. He is the standard. He is who He is, and you believe that. You have even committed to make Him Lord of your life. Period, the end.

Yet, in spite of this strong faith, do you seem to get distracted? I do. Does your life get so busy that you sometimes lose focus on what's most important? Mine does. Do you believe one thing yet entertain other ideas? I do. For instance, do you sometimes turn on the television or computer and get pulled into areas that you know deep down are not where you should be? Be honest . . . it's a common snare.

I am that guy. I've been a Christian for a long time and I know what I believe. It's deep within me. But a part of me is able to turn those convictions on and off. Other things can take the place of my faith.

Over the past decade I have come to two important conclusions about myself:

Conclusion #1: If left to my own devices, I will destroy myself.

That's a pretty harsh reality, wouldn't you say? I mean, really? Can't I live a life that protects what I have been blessed with? My marriage. My kids. My work. My friends. I ask myself and I ask you . . . why would I destroy these things?

But you see, I've noticed that I have the ability to lower and lower my standards. And I'm talking microscopic increments of lowering. So small that each one feels like not such a big deal. But eventually, after all those compromises, I can find myself in a very wrong place. Destroyed.

But don't write me off and stop reading. Here's the second conclusion I have come to:

Conclusion #2: If I put my focus squarely on God, I will be blessed!

That's right . . . if I just do *this one thing*—stay focused on God—I will not be destroyed. In fact, on the contrary, I will be protected. If I stay consistent in seeking Him every day, I will experience peace. My family will experience this too. Because I'm their leader, it is vital that I'm close to God. For their peace. For their protection.

Are you like me in this? Have you also come to these two simple conclusions about yourself? If not, let me clue you in here: They are true for all of us.

So how do we forgetful men stay focused every day? How do we not allow ourselves to get distracted? How do we keep ourselves from checking out spiritually? How do we protect our blessings? How do we avoid forgetting what's most important?

Quite simply, it's about reminders. We need *reminders*. Reminders in different forms. We need friends who remind us. We married guys need our wives to remind us. We need to go to church regularly as a reminder. We need the Bible *every day* as a reminder.

I was so struck with those two basic and contrasting conclusions about myself that I did something a little different as a self-reminder. It's kind of weird, so bear with me here. You know how some people put little Post-it Notes around to remind them of something important? Or how others place pictures of their family on their desk at work, just to keep them in their thoughts? These can be effective reminders. Well, here's what I did. Again, it's a little strange, but I was desperate. Following a gut-wrenching recommitment to Christ that I had made back in the year 1998, I attached a little figurine of Jesus to the dashboard of my car. It's similar to one of those action figures you see kids playing with. Crazy, huh? I don't know . . . I just felt like doing something a little different as a reminder to myself. I saw, all too clearly, how close I had come to total destruction. (Read on; you'll see. I'm not kidding.) I desperately didn't want to go back to what had led me to my recommitment. I wanted protection. *I needed a reminder.*

I invite you to allow this book to serve as a reminder to you. Understand that you can be blessed in ways you never imagined as long as you stay focused on Christ.

Your friend,

Clay

Tie them to your hands and wear them on your forehead as *reminders.* Write them on the doorposts of your house and on your gates.—Deuteronomy 6:8-9

Clay Crosse

Meet Dashboard Jesus

Therefore, I will always be ready to remind you of these things, even though you *already* know *them*, and have been established in the truth which is present with *you*. I consider it right, as long as I am in this *earthly* dwelling, to stir you up by way of reminder.

2 Peter 1:12-13

Dashboard Jesus came my way in the year 1998. The *real* Jesus came into my life eighteen years prior, in 1980. You've got to understand the difference here.

Dashboard Jesus is simply a plastic figurine I attached to the dashboard of my car. The *real* Jesus is . . . well, He's Jesus. You know the guy, right?

Born of a virgin.

Grew up and picked out twelve *normal, everyday, nothing-special* guys to be His followers.

Got extremely famous extremely fast by doing and saying things that no one had seen or heard or even thought about.

Allowed some jealous types to have Him executed.

Came back to life a few days later, causing thousands to drop to their knees in awe.

Said good-bye, went to heaven, and began work on the permanent home for His many followers.

Left His spirit to guide them on earth, leaving some saying, "Wow! Thanks, Jesus!" and others saying, "Huh?"

Plans to come back later for one final globe-rocking.

Yeah . . . that guy. Jesus. The *real* Jesus. Not Dashboard Jesus. Dashboard Jesus is simply there to remind me of the real Jesus.

* * *

I came to know Jesus in 1980. I'll always remember the night I asked Him to forgive me of my sins, come into my life, and be my friend. My Father. My Guide. My Way. My Lord.

Our youth group was on an outreach trip to Missouri. Honestly, my main goal for the trip was not specifically community outreach. I was mostly interested in playing basketball with the guys or looking for a girlfriend to spend time with on the trip. My eyes scanned the immediate horizon for one such young lady. I was young and just discovering how cool girls were.

One night as I scoped out the room for girls, I was blindsided by someone else. Jesus. It was the last thing I was expecting. Our youth leader, John Ellzey, gave nightly talks to our group. On that night, he talked to us about the two different places people go after they die. He explained that everyone will go to either one place or the other. He then told us that if any of us had doubts about where we would go, we could settle that issue right then and there.

He said, "Jesus died on that cross to pay the price for your sin. In doing that, He has offered each of you the gift of salvation and eternity with Him in heaven. All you have to do is say, 'Yes! I accept that gift. Please forgive me of my sins and come into my life. I want to follow You!'"

I sat there thinking about where I would go if I died that night. I was worried. I had real doubts. It was weird because I had always thought I was "saved"—but on that night, I wasn't so sure. I thought back to a time when I was maybe five or six. I remember walking down the aisle with my mom at church. Her filling out some card. Me getting baptized. All that.

But then, years later on our youth trip, I wasn't sure of anything. That action I took as a small child seemed very fuzzy in my mind. I sat there awhile and asked myself, "Am I saved? Really . . . am I? Why do I feel so strange tonight?" I definitely believed in heaven and hell, but I sure didn't know which one I was going to. That night, with complete sincerity, I asked Jesus to forgive me of my sins. I told Him that I believed that He died for my sins, and I asked Him to come into my life.

It felt great. It felt new. It felt right.

When we got home from the trip I walked the aisle (again) at our church, and that night I got baptized (again). This time though . . . I was sure.

Two-Dimensional Christianity

There's a sad misconception out there about having a relationship with Jesus. It goes like this: There are two main moments on the timeline of your relationship with Christ.

1. Come to know Christ.

2. Go to heaven.

That's it!

Get saved . . . . (These dots are your life.)

Then go to heaven . . . .
. . . .
. . . .
. . . . (These dots are eternity.)

It's funny—never does it cross some men's minds that during that first set of dots there should be any real activity with Jesus. They probably think, *I'm saved. That's great.* They must also think, *I'm going to heaven, and that's great too.*

Instead of asking, "Jesus, what are we going to do... *today?*"

* * *

Reminder:

Every day ask, "Jesus, what are we going to do… *today?*"

That was me for much of my early life as a Christian. I thought, *It's so great that I am saved. And even greater that I am going to heaven one day.* Now don't get me wrong. These two core realities are definitely worthy of our thanksgiving. But why didn't I think, *It's great that I can have Jesus go to work with me. And not only there . . . He can go with me everywhere! I can experience every moment of my life . . . with Christ?*

For many years I didn't look at our relationship quite like that.

Finally though, it clicked. One day it clicked that I was supposed to walk with Jesus *throughout my life*. Not just on Sundays. Not just when others are looking. Not just when I'm in emergency mode. And definitely not just when I'm on some stage singing a song about Him.

Always.

So how long do you think it took for this simple reality to sink in with me? A few weeks after I came to know Him in 1980? Maybe a few months? Years? (Have I mentioned that I'm *slow* to learn sometimes?) Try *eighteen* years. That's right! Eighteen years after that night when I asked Jesus to forgive me of my sins. Eighteen years after the night that I invited Him into my life. Eighteen years!

That's a lot of dots.

A Man of God? (Not Really)

The year was 1998. I was cruising along in extreme comfort mode. My life, by most indicators, was perfect. I had a wonderful and beautiful wife, Renee. We had two sweet daughters, ages five and one. My career in Christian music was flying high. I was busy piling up number-one songs and multiple Dove Awards. Offers were streaming in. Interview requests. Cover stories. Concert bookings.

All this was my dream come true. I had imagined just such a life for a long time. But growing up as an aspiring singer I'd known the odds of making it were slim at best. I'd been realistic, accepting that I would probably never actually have that kind of life. I'd work a normal job, and music would simply be a side hobby, I thought. But in the early nineties when it all started to really happen for me, I loved every aspect of it. I got to leave my day job, as a driver for FedEx, to tour full time. I was living my dream.

It felt great. It felt new. It felt right.

But something wasn't right. Specifically . . . me. I wasn't right. I was . . . *off*. Off from what I was supposed to be. Off from what God wanted me to be. Just off. I was so focused on *me* and so focused on *my comfort. My fame. My pleasure.*

That year, though, God reminded me that He was still there and that He still loved me and really wanted my life to be different and even better. He wanted to be close to me, but sadly, we just weren't very close. I was too busy with me. My life was too crammed with my desires to devote any time or energy to Jesus.

God has a variety of ways to get our attention when He knows we need to be reminded to listen to Him. The way He got *my* attention was through my singing voice. Sounds like a strange way to tap me on the shoulder, but I know that's what He was doing—and in retrospect, it was probably the best possible way. I was on the Stained Glass tour with Jaci Velasquez. *Stained Glass* was my third CD release. It was, to some observers, my strongest project to date, and we were all sure that it would only propel me to a higher level of fame and success.

In the middle of that tour, though, something interesting and terrible happened to my voice. I lost it. Maybe not entirely, but there's no doubt that I lost much of my ability. It was so weird. So unreal. I couldn't do the little things vocally that I had been able to do my whole life. I would call Renee from the road and say, "Honey, something's just not right with my voice. I don't know what it is." She would try to encourage me that everything would work out, that it would heal. Others said, "Don't worry, Clay. It will come back." I sure hoped they were right because I was having an extremely hard time trying to get through my concerts.

The weeks turned into months.

This situation upset me like nothing I had ever faced. I was scared to death that I was going to lose this dream life that I had acquired. I had put all my hope in my singing ability, and I was convinced that if I lost it, I would be worthless.

I looked for help at the Vanderbilt Voice Center in Nashville. This place specializes in training, repairing, and maintaining the voices of singers. The doctors there stuck a tiny camera down my throat, and we looked at my vocal cords on a monitor. Truthfully, I was hoping that they would look at them and say, "Ah-ha . . . there it is. You have nodules on your vocal cords. That's the problem. We'll have to do surgery, followed by months of rest. Then you'll be back to your old self."

Isn't that strange? I actually *wanted* them to find a problem so that I could make sense of what I was going through on the road. But no, they didn't see a thing. My vocal cords looked perfectly fine. That should have been good news, but it left me even more confused. I sat there thinking to myself, *What in the world is wrong with my voice? Why can't I sing like I used to?* It was maddening.

From there I made an appointment to see another vocal therapist. A specialist. A vocal coach. I went to Chris Beatty's office and told him all about what was going on with my voice. I had hopes that he would put me on some schedule of vocal exercise and diet that would fix my problem. He sat there and listened as I explained my problem. The whole time I didn't say a thing about my personal life. I just talked about my singing.

I'll never forget the first thing he said.

"Clay, what have you been reading . . . *in the Bible?*"

(pause)

"How's your prayer life?"

(pause)

"Are you serving anywhere? I mean, I know you're out doing concerts, and I hear you on the radio and see you on TV and such. But are you plugged in anywhere really serving?"

(pause)

"And how are you and Renee?"

(pause)

"Clay . . . *are . . . you . . . a . . . man . . . of . . . God?*"

I sat there in stunned silence. Completely speechless. Like a deer frozen in the headlights. Grasping for something . . . anything to say. But I just sat there. Nothing.

Then I felt the tears coming on. You know the feeling. There's just no stopping them. At first you think, *Okay, I'm getting kind of choked up here, but I'll do it quietly. No one has to know. Maybe I'll just get a little misty eyed.* But then you realize that this is deep. Something way inside of you has been directly touched. The tears just start flowing. And you can't do it quietly. There's no way. You just start sobbing.

That was me there in Chris's office. I hadn't known this man for fifteen minutes, and I was sitting there crying my eyes out.

Talk about a wake-up call. Talk about a ground-zero moment. But as it turns out, my meltdown in Chris's office was great for me. I hear you asking, "How can crying like a baby in front of a complete stranger be a great thing?" Well, that moment showed me something. Something I had been blind to. At that moment, I saw that I was far from God and that my life was spiraling out of control. Chris asking me those questions (things I now categorize as Christianity 101–type questions) showed me where I was. And I didn't like where I was. I was far from God. I needed to get closer to Him. And finally, I *wanted* to get closer to Him.

* * *

A Man of God—For Real

At the time of my meeting with Chris Beatty, Renee and I had been married for eight years (and had dated the prior six years). We were close. Very close. We were the kind of couple who thought alike, talked alike, and even looked alike. We finished each other's sentences all the time. We were tight.

Being this close also means that you can't hide much from the other. Oh, you can try, but in the end your partner always knows something's up. It's nonverbal. She just knows.

I couldn't keep Renee in the dark about what I was feeling after my visit with Chris. She could see it in my eyes every day. Something was cooking in my head and heart, and she knew it. One day I finally just blurted out, "Honey, we need to talk." Of all places, we were at church when I told her this. I asked her to get a babysitter that afternoon so we could talk. That alone told her this was serious. "Why do we need to be alone? Just what do we *need* to talk about?" she asked.

That afternoon I just unloaded. I let her know that I needed to change my life. I informed her that our life that seemed perfect . . . was not. I had issues. I had a secret life.

She knew that I had been agonizing about my singing difficulties. She knew how bad that was hurting me. But other than that, she thought everything else was pretty much normal.

I told her, "Renee, I'm a mess. You know that my singing has me very upset, but I am feeling God telling me that my whole life is a mess. And it is." She sat there looking at me, thinking, *What on earth?*

I just had to tell her. It was time to take responsibility. It was time to own up.

"It's my thought life," I said. "It's wrong. It's sinful. Renee, I know that you know about me seeing some porn before we got married. You must have thought, like I did, that it was out of my life since we got married. But, honey, I've got to tell you . . . I have been seeing it again lately."

She just stared at me. There was a deeply sad look on her face. There was anger and hurt. I continued, "Honey, please hear me. I have not committed adultery. There is no one else. It's just that my thought life is driving me in that direction. I can feel it. And if I don't change things, I know that we will be destroyed."

That was the best day of my marriage.

* * *

I hear you saying, "Excuse me . . . did I miss something here? Did he just say that was the *best* day of his marriage? That sounded pretty terrible to me!"

Okay, I'll admit it was tough. Actually, *tough* doesn't really sum up that day. It was wounding on Renee, and it was tough on me too. It hurt. We cried. We screamed. We cussed. We prayed. *What?* Wait a minute now. Let's replay that . . .

They hurt.

They cried.

They screamed.

They cussed.

They *prayed?*

Yes, we prayed. One of those crying-out-to-God prayers, yes, with real tears. One of those "we-need-help!" prayers. More accurately, one of those "I'm-so-messed-up, help-me-God!" prayers.

Here's why I refer to that day as the best day of our

marriage. That afternoon marked the beginning moment of our rededication to Christ. Why do I call it *our* rededication to Christ? After all, it was my problem with porn, not Renee's. It was my failure, not hers. Well, in the weeks and months that followed, we both started to realize that the porn was a symptom of a much deeper problem. I was far from God. That was the problem. And Renee also made that realization about herself. There we were—a Christian couple not where God wanted us to be. We saw clearly that we had been flat-out in love with the world and in love with ourselves and our comfort and had managed to carve out a little life that only had so much room for God.

God's Word was talking to us in a clear way about this:

Don't love the world's ways. Don't love the world's goods. Love of the world squeezes out love for the Father. Practically everything that goes on in the world—wanting your own way, wanting everything for yourself, wanting to appear important—has nothing to do with the Father. It just isolates you from him. The world and all its wanting, wanting, wanting is on the way out—but whoever does what God wants is set for eternity. (1 John 2:16-17, MSG)

This passage (as well as James 4:4, the scripture that begins this chapter) hit me hard. They held a huge mirror in front of me and yelled, "This is you, Clay! This is you!" I could no longer deny that I loved planet Earth. Specifically, I loved our nice little existence in lovely Brentwood, Tennessee. I liked my house . . . too much. I liked my cars . . . too much. I liked my fame . . . too much. I was comfortable, and I wasn't driven to pursue much more than my own happiness.

After my rededication, God started showing me so much. Every area of my life began to change as I started looking for Him more and more. It was amazing. It was life-changing. I felt like a different man. In fact, I recorded a CD and titled it "A Different Man" for this very reason.

It felt great. It felt new. It felt right. Now, more than ever!

Reminders

The months that followed were nothing short of amazing. There were times during that season of my life that I remember praying, *God, I feel so close to You right now, and it feels great! I see clearly what a clown I have been in the past, and now I see just how far Your love has extended to me. Thank You, Father!*

Then I would continue, *But, Lord, I don't want to go back to where I was. I want to stay close to You. I want this fire to keep burning in me. I don't want to lose this. I don't want to get distracted with life and forget this.*

I needed reminders.

Enter Dashboard Jesus!

I wanted something obvious to place in my line of vision. Somewhere I would be on a daily basis. My car! I decided to place a reminder right there in my car, on my dashboard. At first I thought about maybe a little scripture taped there. Not a bad idea. Then I thought maybe a picture of my family. Great idea as well. But eventually I wanted something even more obvious. Then I remembered having seen a little Jesus figurine somewhere. Thank goodness for the Internet, because a few days later there in my mailbox was my own little Dashboard Jesus. I put it in my car and immediately knew that I had done something strange. Something, well…not normal. But I kept it there anyway. (As a side note, it came as a bobblehead, but over time I couldn't stand the bobbling, so I glued it down. Jesus doesn't bobble, does he?)

Yes, I simply put it in my car as an obvious reminder to myself. After all, how much more obvious can you get? That little statue was staring at me. But as I said before, it was just a plastic figurine. I didn't bow down to it. I didn't talk to it, though I did have to look at it. After all, it was right there in my line of sight, and when I saw it, it reminded me of things. Important things.

Things like . . . Jesus is here. Jesus is always with me. The *real* Jesus. He's here. Don't shut Him out. Don't ignore Him. Don't forget Him, Clay. Don't you ever forget Him. Because He certainly won't ever forget you. When you allow Him to be crowded out, when you are far from Him and He's the last thing on your mind, at that very same time He is longing for you and you are centered in His mind.

I'm reminded to take Him with me everywhere I go. I'm reminded not to live a distracted life. I'm reminded to stay focused on Christ. Always.

So many things can capture a man's attention. The distractions go on and on. But the one that tops the list will probably not be a surprise to anyone. For the number-one distraction for pretty much every guy I know (including me), just turn the page to the next chapter.

Don't Forget (Chapter Recap)

If left to our own devices, we can get into a lot of trouble—even if we don't mean to. But if we keep our eyes on God, we will be blessed. I don't know about you, but I'm pretty interested in being blessed by God!

Life is full of distractions, so we have to work at staying focused on God. We need reminders.

Our relationship with God must be more than two dimensional. It's much more than simply asking for salvation, declaring ourselves saved, and then going to heaven at the end of life. We must walk with Jesus every day.

We need reminders. It's up to us to put them in place.

The Number-One Distraction

Anyone who even looks at a woman with lust has already
committed adultery with her in his heart.

Matthew 5:28

You guessed the topic of this chapter already, I'll bet. Let's face
it, God gave men a strong sex drive (for good reasons), but
unless we take it seriously, it can be the number-one distraction
keeping us from Him. It's one of life's little paradoxes: Without
God, it's incredibly difficult to keep from being led astray by
your sexual nature. Yet with God—and a few reminders you
can put in place—it's something you can live well with and not
something that causes harm.

Tale of Two Guys

Two men walk into an airport. These guys don't know each other. They will never meet. But they have a lot in common.

Both men are thirty-four years old. They each have been married for ten years. They each have two children. They both are Christians and attend similar, prominent churches in their hometown.

Brandon is flying to Columbus, Ohio. Seth is flying to Portland, Oregon.

Both of their trips will be short. They'll fly to their destinations. Have business meetings. Then fly home the next morning.

Brandon's Trip

6:00 AM: Alarm goes off. Says a quick *Lord-help-me-today* prayer just before his feet hit the floor.

6:30 AM: Kisses wife bye. Drives to airport. Music blaring.

7:15 AM: Gets to airport. Grabs a newspaper. Notices the attractive women on all the magazine covers. Looks for a second. Snaps out of it. Moves on. Grabs a coffee. Gets on his 8:15 AM flight.

10:00 AM: Lands in Columbus. Goes to baggage claim. Cell phone rings. A friend says, "Hey, man. Just checking in. Let's pray for your day." Brandon says, "Thanks for the prayer, man. I'll call you later." Grabs bag. Hops on the hotel shuttle.

10:30 AM: Sets his bag down in his room. Has a few hours before his meeting. Calls wife, reports: "Traffic wasn't bad this morning. Flight was smooth. No worries . . . except I already miss you." Hangs up. Grabs the remote. Flips channels. Lands on *SportsCenter*. Catches up on all the vital sports news. Resumes channel flipping. Lands on the hotel's menu of movie offerings. Thinks, *Hmmm. A movie tonight might be cool. I'll have a little time later after my meeting.* Notices the categories: Drama, Comedy, Family, and Adult. *Adult*, he thinks. *That doesn't look so great right now. But later on . . . it might.* Something about when the sun goes down, things change. It's weird. Has a second thought and decides to engage the Block Adult Titles option on the menu screen (effectively blocking those titles while he's staying there). Orders room service for lunch. Prepares for his meeting.

1:00 PM: Arrives at the meeting. Sitting at a boardroom table, he meets the group assembled to hear his presentation. He can't help but notice that one is a very good-looking woman. She smiles and seems very friendly toward him. He thinks about her briefly as others talk. Snaps out of it. Thinks of his wife. Gets his game face on. Makes his pitch to the whole group.

4:00 PM: After several individual meetings and a tour of the facility, he and a group, including the smiling woman, head out for an early dinner. At the restaurant, there's the whole "who sits where?" moment before they all sit down. Though something in him wants to, Brandon decides not to sit so close to the smiling, very good-looking woman. The conversation runs the gamut. Brandon tells the group about his wife and kids. Dinner is great. They all shake hands, and he heads back to his room.

6:00 PM: Back at the hotel, he hits the hotel fitness room for some lifting and a little cardio.

7:00 PM: Showers and flips the TV on. Football. Perfect!

10:00 PM: Starts to wind down. Calls his friend from earlier. Talks about his day. They pray, and he says, "Thanks, man. Talk to you later." Phones wife. Reads Bible for a bit. Goes to sleep.

10:00 AM the next day: Arrives home. Kisses wife.

Seth's Trip

6:00 AM: Alarm goes off. Showers.

6:30 AM: Kisses wife bye. Drives to airport. Music blaring.

7:15 AM: Gets to airport. Buys a newspaper and a *Maxim* magazine. Grabs a coffee. Gets on his flight.

11:00 AM: Lands in Portland. Goes to baggage claim. Wife calls. He reports, "Made it here fine. Love you too. Bye." Grabs bag. Hops on hotel shuttle.

11:30 AM: Sets his bag down in his room. Has some time before his meeting. Grabs the remote. Flips channels. Lands on the hotel's menu screen. Sees movie options. Thinks, *Maybe later.* Resumes channel flipping. Hits *SportsCenter.*

Noon: Orders room service for lunch. Prepares for his meeting.

1:00 PM: Arrives at his meeting. Sitting at a boardroom table, he meets the group assembled to hear his presentation. He notices a very good-looking woman. She smiles and crosses her nice legs. He smiles back and thinks about her briefly as others talk: *Wow, she's so hot.* Regains focus. Makes his sales pitch to the whole group.

4:00 PM: After individual meetings and a little tour of the plant, he and a group, including the woman with nice legs, head out for an early dinner. At the restaurant, everyone chooses a seat. No complaints from him when he ends up right next to the smiling, very good-looking woman with nice legs. The conversation runs the gamut. People get loosened up, and jokes start to fly. As the volume increases, Seth and the woman can make little inside jokes back and forth, considering how close they are in proximity. Everyone is enjoying themselves, and dinner is great. A few hours later they all shake hands, and he heads back to his room.

6:00 PM: Back at the hotel, he hits the hotel gym for a little exercise.

7:00 PM: Showers and flips on the TV. Football. Perfect! He sits there watching the game, but it's the strangest thing . . . he can't concentrate on football. He can't stop thinking about that woman he met earlier. *Boy, she was incredible*, he thinks. His thoughts get more and more detailed. *Man, I'll bet she's great in bed*. He begins to imagine how things could easily develop between the two of them on future business trips to Portland.

7:15 PM: His cell phone rings. It's his wife. "Hey, hon. Just checking in. How has your day been going? Things have been a zoo around here. You'll never guess what little Caleb said today in the car." Just your normal husband/wife phone chat. "Okay, I'm tired too. Call me when you land tomorrow. I love you. Bye."

8:30 PM: Feels sort of bad about his previous thoughts of that woman from the meeting. Resumes with the football game. By now though, it's a blowout. Bored, he flips through the *Maxim* magazine lying on the bed. Then he begins surfing channels. Checks out the movie options. Drama, Comedy, Family, Adult.

9:30 PM: Orders a porn movie. Does what one does in such a situation. Goes to sleep.

10:00 AM the next day: Arrives home. Kisses wife.

1:00 PM: At work, Seth's boss asks a group if one of them would agree to make the next trip to Portland. "I know you hate these business trips, but I really need someone to go in a couple of weeks." Seth coyly raises his hand. "What the hey . . . I'll go."

And They All *Didn't* Live Happily Ever After

Do I really need to tell you where this story is headed? Seth goes back to Portland . . . several times. He and the smiling woman get more and more comfortable around each other. They eventually hook up . . . several times. His marriage crumbles to divorce. His kids can now see their dad . . . every other weekend. Nice, huh? Really nice ending to the story.

Maybe you are reading this contrasting tale of two different men and really don't think you relate to these guys, Brandon and Seth. You may be saying, "Man, I don't exactly find myself in boardroom meetings with hot women giving me the eye all that often. And I don't travel a lot. I'm not in hotel rooms alone. That's just not me."

Hey, I understand. The demographic of guys reading this book will vary greatly. You may work out of your home. You may go into an office. Perhaps you work outdoors. You may be between jobs right now. You may work at a church. But you may, like me, find yourself out on the road from time to time.

You may be old or you may be young (whatever those words mean). You may be single. Divorced. Remarried. You may be in a great marriage. You may be in a terrible marriage. You might be well-off financially. You may be in debt up to your eyeballs, scraping by month to month.

You might occasionally look at porn. You may not look at it at all. Porn might not appeal to you. But if you're like a lot of men, it may call out to you often. You may be straight. You may struggle with same-sex attraction. There's no limit to where your mind might try to take you.

The point is this: Wherever you are, whoever you are, *whatever* you are, sexual temptation hits you directly. It's something you have to deal with every day.

If you don't feel any sexual drive, well . . . *hmmm* . . . okay then.

But for the 99.9999 percent of the rest of us . . . it's on! Is it *ever* on!

A Reminder:

Sexual temptation is something you have to deal with every day.

Compare and Contrast

Proverbs 22:3 tells us that "a prudent man sees danger and takes refuge, but the simple keep going and suffer for it" (NIV). In this example . . .

Prudent = wise

Simple = (how can I say this nicely?) not so wise

As we look at Brandon and Seth, it's clear that one is trying to be wise and one is not very concerned. No, Brandon's not perfect. (Who, besides Jesus, is?) But at the very least, Brandon makes efforts throughout his day to be wise, while Seth doesn't make much of an effort at all. The results prove this proverb to be true.

The two different business trips were amazingly alike, but let's run down the glaring differences. These differences appear at eleven distinct moments throughout the men's days.

1. Brandon prayed first thing that morning. No such prayer from Seth.

What better way to start every day than to check in with the Lord and basically tell Him, *Lord, go with me today. I'd rather not do it without You!* (We will further discuss the importance of prayer in a later chapter.)

2. Brandon passed on the airport's sexy magazines. Seth buys one.

Now let's be honest here. Brandon wasn't blind. He saw those magazines, and his eyes may have stayed there a few seconds more than he would like to admit. But something inside reminded him, *Brandon . . . stop.* Seth was different. Thinking it was no big deal, he bought a *Maxim* magazine. *After all,* he thought, *it's not exactly porn.*

Well, is it porn? Really . . . isn't it? Have you ever looked at one of those men's magazines? You know the ones: *Maxim, Vibe, Blender.* Wow. If a porn magazine can be defined as one that sexually arouses the reader, then these magazines definitely qualify. I mean, seriously . . . the images in these magazines would get any red-blooded guy "there." And it's interesting how these magazines have positioned themselves as acceptable/mainstream reading material for men. Since they're not considered porn, men feel okay reading them on flights or in public with relatively no shame.

As the standard of what is and isn't okay seems to get hazier and hazier, Jesus encourages you to keep your standard the same. Always. He said it pretty plainly: "Anyone who even looks at a woman with lust has already committed adultery with her in his heart" (Matthew 5:28).

Plain and simple communication. You've got to love that about Jesus.

So whether society welcomes some magazine, television show, movie, or whatever, our standard should not change. Simply, if it causes me to lust, I should stay away from it. Period. Paul gave Timothy the following advice: "Run from anything that stimulates youthful lusts" (2 Timothy 2:22).

Those *non*porn magazines would stimulate youthful lust in me. No doubt about it. I personally must make a commitment *not* to be an adulterer. If Jesus said just looking and lusting is the same as the physical act, then I've got to go with that too. His standard must be my standard.

3. Brandon's friend phoned and prayed with him. No such call for Seth.

First, I've got to commend Brandon's friend. What a timely and effective reminder this call was for Brandon! He was being a friend here in the truest sense of the word. His call was an intentional act to reach out to Brandon and say, "Let's pray. I know you're on the road, and I know for sure that it's a jungle out there. In every way."

As we look at this closer, we see that this phone call was no accident or coincidence. This call didn't just happen out of the blue. Brandon and his friend have a specific relationship. Structured and very strong. They know each other well. These guys are what are known as *accountability partners*.

> Accountability partner = someone who partners with another who has common goals by checking in and meeting on a regular basis to honestly and openly discuss what's been going on and to pray for each other

It's important to note that the word *goal* is in this definition. So what's the goal of such a relationship? It's simple. The goal is to provide strength. To keep one another accountable for his actions and to keep each other better protected from harm.

Accountability partners meet on a regular basis (I'd suggest every week). Possibly for breakfast or on a lunch break. Nothing long and drawn out. It might start with some light talk. Discuss the weekend's football games or anything of interest. But eventually, in every sit-down, the guys must be committed to talk about some important issues. These talks must include specific questions. Here are some examples of questions that should be asked every time:

> Did you pray and read God's Word this week? How's that going?

> How was church this week? Did you go? What's been going on there? Are you serving?

> How's the fam? The wife and kids? What's been going on there?

> How are your friends? Who have you been hanging out with?

> How have you been tempted this week? How did that go?

> Did you look at a woman in the wrong way? TV? Movies? Any porn? Be honest.

> Did you put yourself in an awkward situation with any woman?

How's the thought life?

Have you been completely honest with me today? Total truth? You're not holding anything back from me, are you?

How can I pray for you this coming week?

In addition to these questions, each guy should add questions that pinpoint his specific needs. They should be directly about how he needs prayer and support. In fact, each accountability partner should *provide* the exact questions that he knows deep down need to be asked of him each week. Spot-on specific things like . . . *So how have things been lately with that new good-looking intern at your work? You know . . . the one you were telling me about.* The questions need to be that personal and apply to the person's life.

A Reminder:

Accountability partners are vital. Make sure he knows exactly what your weaknesses are.

There are two main requirements for an accountability relationship: maturity and honesty. First, each guy must be mature enough to commit to weekly or regular meetings. It's a lot to ask someone to meet you every week on an ongoing basis. It takes someone who has the same goals as you in this effort.

Second, honesty is an absolute must. If you're not going to be honest, then don't even bother. It will be a waste of time and breath. Think about it. If a guy is doing these meetings but lying about his life, then what good is that? What a joke. Why do it at all? It's the honesty in these relationships that provides the real power. When two guys are committed to seriously helping each other and praying for each other, great things are accomplished. The relationship must be totally up-front and aboveboard. The power of these meetings is in knowing that being truthful will push each guy to live a purer life during the week.

You may have heard of this kind of relationship and thought, like most guys, *Hmmm . . . this sounds okay, but accountability is just not for me.* Hey, that's understandable. Guys don't want to get real with someone else. We like to keep things private. We would rather it look like everything's under control—and having an accountability partner says, "Hey, I'll admit it. I need a little help here." It flies in the face of the traditional strong, proud, invincible-male thinking. Guys tend to think, *If there's a problem, I'll fix it . . . on my own.*

Don't be that guy. Let me tell you this straight up. *You need an accountability partner! I need an accountability partner! If you don't have one, get an accountability partner.* "You use steel to sharpen steel, and one friend sharpens another" (Proverbs 27:17, MSG). Having an accountability partner will make you stronger. Don't you want that? Sure you do! Having an accountability partner will offer protection. Who doesn't need that? I know I do. We all do. Having an accountability partner will help you be the man God wants you to be.

4. Brandon calls his wife from baggage claim. Seth's wife calls him.

There's a huge difference here. Ask any woman, and she'll agree that there is a big difference in whether her husband makes the call or if she has to call her husband. If you call her, you're saying, "I care about you and what's going on with you." Her calling you doesn't really say that, now does it?

If you're a husband . . . man, she wants to know that you give a rip. It's clear to her, and others, what's precious to you. She sees you get excited about good things going on in your career. She sees you jump up and down and act crazy for your favorite sports teams. She knows what does it for you, and believe me, she desperately wants to know that she's precious to you.

Just like in Song of Songs, she wants to believe that you think,

There's no one like her on earth,

never has been, never will be.

She's a woman beyond compare.

My dove is perfection. (6:8, MSG)

She wants to know that you are strongly pursuing her. Solomon wrote,

> Ah, I hear my lover coming!
>
> He is leaping over the mountains,
>
> bounding over the hills. (Song of Songs 2:8)

She wants to know that you took the effort to call her. And that you are there, on the other end of that phone, thinking of her and loving her. Take a few seconds here and there. Give her a call. Remind her. Remind yourself!

* * *

A Reminder: Check in with your wife. This simple caretaking act will reap enormous benefits.

5. Brandon cancels the adult titles from his hotel movie-menu options. Seth does not.

Brandon does a very wise thing here. He looks ahead a few hours and puts up some defense on the front end. He's being honest with himself and admitting that later on that night, he might think about ordering a porn movie. Nice move, Brandon. Wise move.

6. Brandon clearly notices the attractive woman at his meeting but redirects his thoughts to his wife. Seth notices the woman at his meeting and keeps on thinking about her.

Seth lets his thoughts run a little wild. He sits there and imagines all sorts of things he'd like to do with that woman. Honestly, it's easy to do. Our imaginations are incredibly strong and well created. And like anything, they can be used for good or evil. Our imaginations have amazing capacity to look at a fully clothed woman and completely undress her in our minds. And the thoughts just go and go and go . . . *if we let them.*

Jesus spoke of our thoughts and how powerful they are.

> It is what comes from inside that defiles you. For from within, out of a person's heart, come evil thoughts, sexual immorality, theft, murder, adultery, greed, wickedness, deceit, lustful desires, envy, slander, pride, and foolishness. All these vile things come from within; they are what defile you. (Mark 7:20-23)

7. Brandon decides not to sit by the woman at dinner. Seth makes no attempt to avoid sitting by the woman at dinner.

We go back to that simple proverb again here: "A prudent man sees danger and takes refuge, but the simple keep going and suffer for it" (Proverbs 22:3, NIV). Brandon understands that he really doesn't know this woman and that he should keep it that way. Seth thinks, *What's the harm? After all, it's just dinner.* As the story unfolds, we see that the harm is devastating. And it all started with a simple decision about where to sit at a meal.

8. Brandon brings up his wife and family in conversation at dinner. Seth never goes there.

This is Brandon's reminder to himself, and everyone there, that he has a wife and kids whom he loves. A subtle move but very strong. And very wise.

9. Brandon calls his accountability partner later that evening. Seth . . . no.

Accountability . . . *again.* This is nothing short of *huge.*

10. Brandon calls his wife again. Seth's wife calls him... again.

Just another "Hey, hon. How was your day? I love you. I miss you." Also *huge.*

11. Brandon cracks open his Bible before going to sleep. Seth . . . nope.

This one is as vital as it gets. Brandon closing out his day by opening the Bible is the essence of wisdom. The last thing he's putting in his mind before he goes to sleep is God's truth. (We'll look into this more in a later chapter.)

What's Important to You?

Each of the eleven moments listed here was a time for Brandon and Seth to make a decision. In short, each time they should have been asking themselves, *What am I going to do here?* I think we'd agree that Brandon did indeed ask this question throughout his day. It's doubtful, though, whether Seth considered these moments very important. Their life results show clearly how their actions (and nonactions) affected them.

* * *

A Reminder: Your sexual drive is so strong that without God's help, it will likely overpower you.

I encourage you to think seriously about your actions every day. Are you placing reminders throughout your life to point you in the direction God wants you to go? Do you understand that your sexual drive is superstrong and that without God in your life, it will likely overpower you? Are you willing to intentionally place reminders all throughout your life that will point you to purity?

Reminders like . . .

Prayer (every day)

The Bible (every day)

An accountability partner (every week)

These three reminders are paramount in the life of every man. We've got to have them. All three keep our overall focus aimed in the right direction. More accurately, they remind us of one person: Jesus.

Jesus isn't in the dark when it comes to our desire for sex. He understands it. He gets it. Jesus is perfectly aware of how we are wired. He knows *precisely* what makes us tick. He understands how we are tempted by images, sounds, and people everywhere. Remember, He created us. Our wiring is no mystery to Him. On top of this though, He understands because He was a man; there was a time when He felt the same urges that we do.

"No!" you say. "Not Jesus! There's no way He struggled with the things I struggle with!" Well, He didn't fall to them, but He had thoughts. "This High Priest of ours understands our weaknesses, for he faced *all of the same testings we do*, yet he did not sin" (Hebrews 4:15). When I read in the Bible that Jesus faced "all of the same testings we do," I take that for exactly what it says. Yes, Jesus understands. And the comforting thing is, He offers strength for us.

> The eyes of the LORD search the whole earth in order to strengthen those whose hearts are fully committed to him. (2 Chronicles 16:9)

> For I can do everything through Christ, who gives me strength. (Philippians 4:13)

Remember these verses. They are promises from your Father in heaven who gets what you are going through. When you feel weak, when you feel too far gone, when you get sick and tired of caving, when you feel helpless, remember these promises.

Don't Forget (A Recap)

Your sex drive is one of the strongest distractions you'll face in your quest to be a man after God's own heart. Get this under control because the potential for disaster is real.

You have to seek wisdom in order to find it. And you have to put reminders in place to keep you from getting distracted by life.

The three most powerful reminders you can give yourself are prayer (do it every day), the Bible (read it every day), and an accountability partner (meet weekly).

You need an accountability partner. If you don't have one, get one! Having an accountability partner will make you stronger and more protected. Get real. Get accountable. Get strong.

Relationships have to be maintained. This means your relationship with God, of course, but it also means your relationship with family, friends, your children, and your wife. Taking the lead in maintaining the connection shows that it's important to you. *Especially* when it's your relationship with your wife.

As in the Song of Songs, she wants to believe that you think "there's no one like her on earth, never has been, never will be. She's a woman beyond compare" (6:8, MSG). And she wants to know that you are strongly pursuing her, as Solomon wrote: "Ah, I hear my lover coming! He is leaping over the mountains, bounding over the hills" (Song of Songs 2:8). She wants to know that you care enough to touch base with her. So do it!

God truly understands the challenges you face because He was on earth as a man and faced them too. And He promises to help you. He's on your side! "I can do all things through Christ who strengthens me"

Dashboard Jesus

(Philippians 4:13, NKJV).

* * *

Clay Crosse

Uhh . . . I'm Not

Much of a Reader

All Scripture is inspired by God and is useful to teach us what is true and to make us realize what is wrong in our lives. It corrects us when we are wrong and teaches us to do what is right. God uses it to prepare and equip his people to do every good work.

2 Timothy 3:16-17

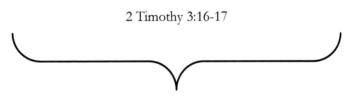

When I'm out on the road speaking or singing somewhere, I am floored by the number of guys who walk up to me and say, "Man, I'd love to read your books, but I'm just not much of a reader." I look at them and nod my head to convey, "I hear ya, bro," but inside I'm thinking, *Did he really just tell me that?* He may as well have said, "Uhh . . . I ain't too smart."

Believe me here; I don't care that these guys haven't read *my* books, per se. It's just that they aren't reading *any* books. And most alarming, they are telling me that they are not reading *the* book—God's Word. The Bible.

The Ultimate Owner's Manual

When so many men unashamedly tell me they don't read the Bible, they are making a statement about how we, as Christian men, have regressed. What in the world are we doing? Working? Yes. Most guys I know are pretty serious about their jobs. But I ask myself, *After work, what are they into then?* Watching TV? Yes. A lot. A whole lot of TV watching going on I'm sure . Checking e-mail and surfing online? Sure. Working out/running/exercising? Some do, sure. Playing golf? Uh-huh. Playing video games? Some guys do. Sitting around eating? Yes, probably too much. Hanging with friends and family? Sure.

Here's the thing. None of these activities is a sin. But each can be a real problem, and a sin, if it becomes more important than God's Word. These activities can collectively push Him out of our lives.

A lot of men get to the end of the day and are just plain tired. Mentally and physically tired. They've worked all day and just want to get home and chill. They sit down and watch TV. Maybe they take a nap. Something relaxing. Just to escape. The last thing they want to do is read the Bible.

Guys, hear me on this. (I'll say it slow.)

*We…must…be…in…God's Word…*every day.

Christian man, read your Bible *every day.* It's God's voice.

A Reminder: To really know God, you have to physically open the Bible and read what He has to say . . . for yourself.

We must know this: The Bible is our *only* guidebook. The *only* user's manual. The *only* how-to guide. There is nothing else. All else is foolishness and destruction. But His Word . . . *wow!* His Word . . . it is life. It is joy. It is power. It is perfectly solid. It tells us, "For the word of God is alive and powerful. It is sharper than the sharpest two-edged sword, cutting between soul and spirit, between joint and marrow. It exposes our innermost thoughts and desires" (Hebrews 4:12).

Where to Start?

Ever open the Bible to a random place and blindly point to a verse, just to see what it says? I heard of a guy who did this, and the first verse he pointed to said, "Judas went away and hanged himself."[i] Finding that interesting, he closed the Bible and tried again. The next random verse he pointed to said, "Go and do likewise."[ii] This freaked him out, and he was afraid to try that method again.

There are better ways! A lot of guys just don't know where to start in their Bible reading. After all, it's a big, big book. The Bible contains 66 books; 1,189 chapters; 31,173 verses, and 774,746 words.[vii] Depending on print size, a Bible can be anywhere from 1,500 to 3,000 pages long. That's a lot of book! Not your typical Grisham novel. Not the kind of book you will read over the weekend.

The sheer size of the Bible overwhelms many men when they pick it up—the actual weight (in pounds and ounces) and the weight of the words themselves. It's downright intimidating. Daunting. And since it's not exactly an easy read and they don't know where to begin, most guys never really open it at all. "After all, I'm not much of a reader," they say. TV is easier. *Not reading* . . . that's easier.

I've got to admit, that used to be me. When it came to reading the Bible, I used to think that way. I figured that I knew all the Bible stories, so why should I keep opening a book that I had already heard at church over the years? Then my vocal coach, Chris Beatty, challenged me to open the Bible *every day.*

Yes, every day.

Chris asked me what I was reading, and when I didn't have much of an answer, he gave me a read-through-the-Bible-in-a-year guide. It was simple, like a calendar. Each day contained about a hundred verses—a combination of a passage in the Old Testament, a passage from the New Testament, a psalm, and a proverb. (The whole thing took about fifteen or twenty minutes to read each day.)

I began reading and was so thankful that Chris had handed me that simple guide. It kept me focused. It gave me a daily goal. And it broke the Bible down into something I could manage.

You can download a free printable guide at OneYearBibleOnline.com. If you are having difficulty getting started, I strongly suggest printing off this guide. You can mark off each day as you go. At the end of one year—*boom!*—you will have read all the way through. And believe me, you will feel the effects. This I guarantee. You will be glad you started and glad you stayed with it. If you are like me, you will think, *Wow, that wasn't rocket science. All I did was start reading my Bible—and my life changed for the better.*

* * *

A Reminder: Get serious and follow a plan to read the Bible every day. It will change your life!

Hear me on this; if you don't get anything else from this book you're holding, I want you to get this. *We must be in God's Word.* If you print off the OneYearBibleOnline.com reading guide and start doing it, I wouldn't care if you tossed this book in the trash because you would be on the perfect path to wisdom. The Bible should be your perfect reminder (not *Dashboard Jesus*).

Five Is Not Such a Big Number

The more you read the Bible, the easier it will be. It will become clearer to you that the message of Scripture is not as difficult to grasp as you once thought. Sure, it's heavy—both in actual pounds and content—but it is designed for our minds and hearts to soak it in *with ease*. It's huge, but it's really not thousands of different unassociated stories and thoughts. Fact is, the Bible offers *five* basic themes, consistently recurring in every passage of Scripture.[iii]

Not thousands. Just five. And they are:

The character of God

Judgment for sin

Blessing for faith and obedience

Jesus as Lord and Savior and sacrifice for sin

5. The coming kingdom and glory

That's right. In every passage of Scripture, you will find one (or a combination) of these five themes. What you read in the Bible will always be referencing these things:

Who God is.

He is serious about sin.

He notices and blesses obedience.

Jesus, our Lord, saved us.

Heaven awaits.

Isn't that simple? I mean, really . . . five points. Understanding these main points helps me as I read God's

Word. I know that God is speaking to me, and He will be communicating from this short list of themes. God wants me to hear His Word, and He doesn't want the process of reading to stress me out or be beyond my capability. In short, He wants His Word in me, and He has made that doable (even for the guys who say "I'm not much of a reader.").

* * *

Admit It—We All Need a Little Help

My friend Chris Beatty helped me out a lot by giving me that reading guide. I needed the help back then (and I still do). Don't be ashamed to admit that you could use a little help from someone further down the path with God than you happen to find yourself. Look for a Bible study or a men's group that gets together to discuss the Bible. There are so many great men's groups springing up. I encourage you to plug in to good leadership and lean on another man (or men) to help you grow. It's nothing at all to be ashamed of; in fact, it's biblical and wise.

> Philip ran over and heard the man reading from the prophet Isaiah. Philip asked, "Do you understand what you are reading?"

> The man replied, "How can I, unless someone instructs me?" And he urged Philip to

come up into the carriage and sit with him. (Acts 8:30-31)

Yes, the Bible is big, but don't be intimidated. Yes, it is heavy, but you can do it. The Bible is reliable and usable and absolutely vital for every man. Don't be afraid to ask for help, and find time to open it every day. You can and you should! Like I said, if you only get one thing from this book you are holding, then get this: *Read God's Word every day of your life.*

* * *

A Reminder: It's easy to develop a habit of Bible reading if you get involved with a Bible-study group.

Feeling a Little Wobbly? Check Your Foundation

I used to be that guy whose life seemed perfect. Seriously, I had the world by the tail, as they say. I had a beautiful wife and children. I was making a good living. I had a nice house and nice cars. I had success in my line of work. My family was healthy. Things must have looked good to the outside observer.

But back then I never read the Bible. *Never.*

For that reason, my life was off center. Oh, it looked good, but it wasn't. It wasn't even *okay*. In fact, it was downright shaky, and I was very close to being completely destroyed. The foundation of my life was being supplied by all the wrong things. My foundation wasn't the least bit solid. It was shaky, and I was all about to fall in.

When I rededicated my life to Christ in 1998, I started to read God's Word like never before. This simple daily act transformed me. It surprised me. I finally got it. Throughout my life I had heard about the power of God's Word, but I had never tapped into it. When I finally did, two things hit me at the same time: regret and hope. Regret about how long it took me to wise up, but great hope for a future relying totally on God and His Word.

A lot of Christian men I meet relate to my story. They have a life that *seems* okay. Maybe even better than okay. They have the things that most men think they need to be successful. Yet something just doesn't feel right. They lie in bed at night and wonder, *What am I missing here? Why am I not satisfied? What's wrong with me?*

And while they ask this (or pray this), somewhere near

their bed sits a seldom-opened Bible. Perhaps unintentionally, these men have replaced God's Word with other things that they have come to believe will provide a strong life. But the truth is, those other things will only provide a shoddy foundation. It may feel strong for a while, but eventually it will cause their lives to crumble.

Examples of Shoddy Foundations:

Financial security

Good health

Kids getting good grades

Kids excelling in sports and other things worth bragging about

"Happy" wife

Good appearance

Now don't get me wrong. There is nothing wrong with these things. I want them in my life and so do most guys. These goals aren't, in themselves, sinful. But where they can cause sin is when we think that they—without God—can provide us with what we need. It's easy to think, *If I have these things, I'll be just fine.*

We must make God's Word *the* foundation for our lives. We must not ignore it. We must not think, *Oh, I know all the Bible stories. I've read it before. I can live without reading it regularly.* We must continue to ask God, *What do You have for me* today?

Show me today.

> These words I speak to you are not incidental additions to your life, homeowner improvements to your standard of living. They are foundational words, words to build a life on. If you work these words into your life, you are like a smart carpenter who built his house on solid rock. Rain poured down, the river flooded, a tornado hit—but nothing moved that house. It was fixed to the rock. (Matthew 7:24-25, MSG)

Don't forget to tend to your foundation, and don't get caught up in the trap of building your foundation out of shoddy material. God's Word is the safest place to build your life.

* * *

A Reminder: Don't forget to tend to your foundation, and don't get caught up in the trap of building your foundation out of shoddy material. God's Word is the strongest place to build your life.

In a Tight Spot? Do Like Jesus

Stress. We all feel it. Every one of us. It's a high-pressure world, and most guys are right smack in the epicenter every day. The phrase "it's a jungle out there" certainly applies. And in that jungle, Christian men encounter situations in which they must either stand up for what is biblically right or give in and not respond as God wants them to.

Every man finds himself in a tight spot from time to time. Possibly a confrontation at work. Possibly you are struggling with a moral debate and don't know exactly what to do. Maybe it's a battle at home with the kids or your wife. Maybe a flare-up with extended family (in-laws, grandparents, siblings). Could be that a friend or associate is pulling your chain, and you just want to explode. These situations can cause great stress and if we're not careful they can cause a moral distraction that could easily cause a man to react in a way he'll regret later.

We must rely on God's Word for every big (or little) challenge that comes our way. Jesus did this time and time again. When He found Himself in a bind, what did He do? He pulled out the Word.

One such occasion was when the Pharisees accused Him and His disciples of breaking the Sabbath. This was a serious offense the Pharisees were wrongly trying to bring against Him.[iv] When confronted, Jesus went straight to the Scriptures for undisputable defense.

> At about that time Jesus was walking through some grainfields on the Sabbath. His disciples were hungry, so they began breaking off some heads of grain and eating them. But some Pharisees saw them do it and protested, "Look, your disciples are breaking the law by harvesting grain on the Sabbath."

Jesus said to them, "Haven't you read in the Scriptures what David did when he and his companions were hungry? He went into the house of God, and he and his companions broke the law by eating the sacred loaves of bread that only the priests are allowed to eat. And haven't you read in the law of Moses that the priests on duty in the Temple may work on the Sabbath? I tell you, there is one here who is even greater than the Temple!" (Matthew 12:1-6)

Let's look at this passage for a moment. Have you ever heard of someone making a dangerously bold statement? Jesus looked these guys in the eye and said, "I'm bigger than the Temple." That was bold. That was big. They could have dragged Him away immediately for that statement.

But they just stood there in shock. They listened as He pulled an obscure reference out of scripture. He quoted a minor prophet who was on the scene 750 years prior. Hosea.

Jesus knew the Word and loved the Word and relied on the Word. He referenced Hosea 6:6 when He told the Pharisees, "But you would not have condemned my innocent disciples if you knew the meaning of this Scripture: 'I want you to show mercy, not offer sacrifices.' For the Son of Man is Lord, even over the Sabbath!" (Matthew 12:7-8).

Did you catch that? He threw in another bold zinger with that "I am master of the Sabbath" bit. Understand, those were unthinkable words for a man to utter. Completely outrageous. Try to imagine a man today walking up to the White House and saying, "I am master of this house. I have authority over this house, the Pentagon, and everything else, for that matter." We'd probably see the guy all over the web and TV. They would carry him off in handcuffs. They would say he was insane and lock him up.

Jesus was claiming His rule over the holy temple and the Sabbath! A seemingly crazy statement. The thing is, the Pharisees knew Jesus wasn't insane. He had a strange power and peace like they had never seen. And He had a very loyal and vocal following whose numbers were growing every day. It was undeniable that this guy was something special, and that drove the Pharisees mad with jealousy.

His run-in with the Pharisees was surely a tough situation for Jesus. A tight spot. But He didn't raise His fists. He didn't exhibit superhuman speed and dart out of there. He didn't turn them to stone. He simply quoted a prophet from centuries before. And there, in that moment, the prophet's words (God's Word) brought the undeniable truth.

* * *

Job also found himself in a tough spot. Actually, his situation went well beyond that—he wasn't in a little jam that could be quickly remedied. No, this guy was devastated. Out of nowhere . . . *boom!* Life as he had known it was taken from him. He was all but destroyed. One minute he was very wealthy, and in the next he lost everything he had worked so hard to acquire.

I think, *what if that happened to me?* I'm not wealthy like Job, but I think about such a thing happening in my life. If tomorrow all my earthly possessions were taken, I've got to say I'd be upset. Not that I'm in love with my possessions . . . but let's be real here, it would be terrible. Yet deep down I know that if I still had my family I'd be okay. It would be tough, no doubt about it. But I'd have my wife and children, who are precious to me. I'd be able to look at my loved ones and know that I had not really lost anything—because I would still have them.

But as we know, Job did lose his family (all his children). In one fell swoop, his kids were dead. That's an unbearable thought for any good dad. In fact, it's a thought that we avoid and shut out of our minds. Just the idea one of our children dying is almost unbearable. We know we would be beyond our own ability to cope with the crushing blow of losing a child. We would have to rely on God to carry us through such a time of loss. And that's what Job was experiencing.

Then, adding insult to injury, the guy came down with a severe skin disease that kept him in maddening pain. Nice day, huh?

The opening of the book of Job describes him as a man who "was honest inside and out, a man of his word, who was totally devoted to God and hated evil with a passion" (1:1, MSG). He was clearly a solid citizen, a respected man who was focused on God. But Satan was convinced that this solid man would cave if God allowed these painful things to happen to him.

Incredibly though, Job did *not* buckle under the pressure. Oh, don't get me wrong here—he wasn't perfect. Battling insanity from the severe grief and physical pain, he said some crazy things. He complained. He moaned. He cried. He wished he had never been born. And on top of this, he had to endure some pretty sorry advice and analysis from his friends and his wife. That's right; while he was suffering, they were ripping him verbally.

But in the end, he was able to say, "I have not departed from his commands, *but have treasured his words more than daily food*" (Job 23:12). What an amazing statement in the midst of all he was going through. Despite all he had faced, he still could see that God was his only hope. The story ends with God restoring Job back to his original place, with a family, wealth, and a long life.

A Reminder:

The Bible has wisdom and comfort for times of

Dashboard Jesus

trouble.

Memorize passages so you'll always have Scripture close at hand.

Are you regularly stressed out or finding yourself in a bind? If so, you are normal. You live in the same pressure-cooker world we all do. The challenge, as a Christian man, is to keep the Bible close to you at all times. To have it in your mind when you don't physically have it in your hands. After all, you probably don't walk around the workplace or classroom with your Bible in hand. So hide it in your heart and completely rely on its truth to be your guide in every situation.

Tired of Buckling Under Temptation? Do Like Jesus

Let's face it; we all feel temptation. The book of James even goes as far as to say that we are "blessed" to endure temptation

(1:12, NIV). Blessed? Really?

Yes . . . blessed.

If you're like me, being tempted doesn't feel like much of a blessing. Frankly, I just wish it would go away. My temptations seem to get in the way of everything I know I need to be doing. The things God wants me to be doing. I feel like I could be so much more effective for God if I didn't have those nagging thoughts.

But sure enough, those lures are there for all of us, and God is telling us that we are blessed to have them and endure them. He blesses us because He loves us. It's interesting to see that God didn't shortchange Jesus in any aspect of the human experience. He even blessed Jesus, His own Son, with temptation.

Out in the hot desert, after fasting for forty days (Forty days . . . wow. We'll come back to this in the next chapter.), Jesus was tempted by Satan. Understand that it was the enemy who was doing the tempting. That's always where the temptations in our lives come from. From Satan, our enemy. Not from God, our loving Father (see James 1:13).

Satan threw three attractive lures at Jesus. First, he tempted Jesus with food. This was pretty crafty because Jesus must have been famished after going without food for forty days. Jesus responded,

No! The Scriptures say,

"People do not live by bread alone,

> but by every word that comes from the mouth of God." (Matthew 4:4)

Next, Satan took Jesus into the city of Jerusalem. Trying to tap into Jesus' desire to be noticed, to be famous (nice try, Satan), he suggested that Jesus do some outrageous stunt like jumping off the highest point of the temple. Satan even went so far as to quote Scripture himself in his challenge. Satan said,

> If you are the Son of God, jump off! For the Scriptures say,

> "He will order his angels to protect you.

> And they will hold you up with their hands

> so you won't even hurt your foot on a stone." (Matthew 4:6)[v]

Basically Satan was saying, "Man, let me handle Your publicity. This stunt will be tomorrow morning's biggest watercooler talk. Everyone will hear about You because of this. It'll go viral! You'll be huge! You need this." To this silly idea, Jesus calmly responded, "The Scriptures also say, 'You must not test the LORD, your God'" (Matthew 4:7).

At this point we can see that Satan was frantic and had nearly run out of ideas. The only thing left was to offer Jesus something so big that no man could possibly refuse. So Satan offered Jesus the world on a platter. That's right, he offered to give Jesus all the nations of the world. He told Jesus, "I will give it all to you . . . if you will kneel down and worship me" (Matthew 4:9). But Jesus knew His Scripture, and He clung to it in this time of extreme temptation.

> "Get out of here, Satan," Jesus told him. "For the Scriptures say,
>
> 'You must worship the LORD your God
>
> and serve only him.'" (Matthew 4:10)

Satan got out of there.

Each of Jesus' three responses in this series of temptations comes from the book of Deuteronomy (8:3; 6:16; and 6:13-14). He was applying situations that the Israelites faced in the wilderness to His own wilderness battle with Satan.[vi]

Here's some great news: We can do the same thing today! When we get slammed with some out-of-nowhere temptation—maybe a lustful thought creeps in, maybe an opportunity to falsely slant the numbers in your favor, possibly the thought of calling in sick when you feel fine—we can do what Jesus did. We are tempted to sin; that's a given. And the possibilities for sins, large and small, are endless.

In those moments, have Scripture ready. Do like Jesus did. Fire it off right there. Out loud if possible, or silently in your head if need be. But be ready to directly quote God's

Word. Satan is one powerful being, but quoting Scripture causes him to run like a frightened little girl.

Here are some examples of good verses to fire off. But understand, you must have them in your memory, ready to use for your future protection.

> Since he himself has gone through suffering and testing, he is able to help us when we are being tested. (Hebrews 2:18)

> The eyes of the LORD search the whole earth in order to strengthen those whose hearts are fully committed to him. (2 Chronicles 16:9)

> How can a young person stay pure?

> By obeying your word. (Psalm 119:9)

> You do not belong to yourself, for God bought you with a high price. So you must honor God with your body. (1 Corinthians 6:19-20)

Do like Jesus. Speak God's Word to fight off temptation.

* * *

This Is Your Story

Well-known Bible commentator John MacArthur has written vast studies of the Bible while pastoring Grace Community

Church in Sun Valley, California. His commentaries are some of the most read and highly respected works available. When asked to write a short quote about the Bible as a whole, he stated: "Christian—this is your story. It is from God for you—about you. It tells what He planned for you, why He made you, what you were, what you have become in Christ, and what He has prepared for you in eternal glory."[vii]

I love that. MacArthur's description simplifies things in a way that defines the Bible as not just some book of stories from long ago. Not just some book about other people. No, it is *our story*. As Christians, it is *our* guidebook. *Our* survival manual. It holds the only code for *our* victory. It tells of *our* history as well as *our* promise of the future. It answers the simple question any Christian must ask: "Where did I come from, and where am I going?" On top of that it answers the next question, too: "How should I act on my specific and personal road to getting there?"

As we read the Bible, we should never disconnect from the truth that it is God talking to us as we read. This book has a living author, and He's communicating with you! It's not simply tales from the past that may or may not apply to us. No! It's God talking to us right now. Every time.

He must be on our minds every time we read His Word. To view the Bible as just a nice collection of stories and good ideas is to remove the true power of the words. Its power comes from the fact that God speaks directly to us as we read: "When you received [God's] message from us, you didn't think of our words as mere human ideas. You accepted what we said as the very word of God—which, of course, it is. And this word continues to work in you who believe" (1 Thessalonians 2:13).

Half-Truth?

There are a lot of smart people around the world who are convinced that they have it all figured out. And if there's something they can't wrap their heads around, then it must not exist, they think. These "intellectuals" try to convince others that the miracles in the Bible are simply made-up stories designed to get a larger point across. Just dramatic stories of fiction. Attention-getters. They say that the authors added things after the fact to spice up the Bible stories. Things like talking snakes and donkeys. Burning bushes. Food falling from the sky. A virgin giving birth. Guys walking on top of water. Dead people coming to life. These things, some experts say, could never have happened.

To this we, as Christian men, must say, "Hogwash!" That's the word, a southern term, that comes to mind when I hear people saying that any part of the Bible is not true.

We should either believe the whole book or look at it as a fictional and false account altogether. And of course, that's just not the case. Think about it this way: Would we respect someone if he told the truth part of the time but just made-up stories the rest of the time? No, we would not respect such a person. After a while, we would question every word out of his mouth. Every time he spoke, we would have some degree of doubt. The same applies to the Bible—either it is or it isn't. As followers of Christ, we must proclaim, "*It is!* Father, Your Word *is true!*" Even the wild, outrageous, scandalous, amazing, unthinkable, unusual, otherworldly, far-fetched, and impossible parts. The stuff beyond our limited minds. Because, you see, God is all those things. He's not normal. He's not tame. He's not boring. He's certainly not predictable. We can't calculate the probability of His actions. There's just no way. He is God, and His book is beyond our calculations and charts. To Him, *miraculous* and *unimaginable* are an everyday thing.

You don't have to look hard to find where Jesus landed on the miracles debate. He clearly believed the Bible's miracles to be true, and He spoke of them often. Dana Key, pastor of TLC Church, offered some prime examples of disputed miracles and direct quotes from Jesus about them.[viii]

> About Jonah and the fish, Jesus said, "For as Jonah was in the belly of the great fish for three days and three nights, so will the Son of Man be in the heart of the earth for three days and three nights" (Matthew 12:40).

> About Creation/Adam and Eve, He said, "God made them male and female' from the beginning of creation" (Mark 10:6).

> About Moses and the burning bush, "Haven't you ever read about this in the writings of Moses, in the story of the

burning bush?" (Mark 12:26).

And of the manna sent from heaven, He said, "I tell you the truth, Moses didn't give you bread from heaven. My Father did" (John 6:32).

Just like Jesus did, we must also believe the Bible. The whole Bible. Every part.

* * *

I think we'd all agree, you don't have to look too far in our society to see that there's plenty of false information flying around out there:

> Folks speaking out of both sides of their mouths

> Sketchy talk

> Politicians saying what they think we want to hear

> Little white lies

> Cover-ups

> Fibs

> Fudging

> Smiling faces

Hearty hand shakers

Backslappers

Come-ons

Under-the-table deals

The old bait and switch

Smooth talkers

Constant upselling

Confusing fine print

Rip-offs

Partial truths

Fuzzy math

Let's face it; our world is full of lies, but no lies are in the Bible. And no fables either. The Bible is solid. It is airtight. It is truth. It is God's Word. "For we were not making up clever stories when we told you about the powerful coming of our Lord Jesus Christ. We saw his majestic splendor with our own eyes" (2 Peter 1:16).

Be Like Jesus: Get Serious About the Word of God

Jesus told His followers,

But you need to know that whoever puts me
off, refusing to take in what I'm saying, is
willfully choosing rejection. The Word, the
Word-made-flesh that I have spoken and that I
am, that Word and no other is the last word.
I'm not making any of this up on my own. The
Father who sent me gave me orders, told me
what to say and how to say it. And I know
exactly what his command produces: real and
eternal life. That's all I have to say. What the
Father told me, I tell you. (John 12:48-50, MSG)

There's no debate here. Jesus was serious about the Word of
God. After all, this was His Father's Word. This *is* His Father's
Word. It is *our* Father's Word.

A Reminder:

What would Jesus do? It's
more than a catchy slogan.
It should be our way of life
as Christian men.

So much of this chapter screams, "Do like Jesus!" A few years ago those WWJD (What Would Jesus Do?) bracelets were popular. I suppose it was just a fad, but truly they were on to something. It's how we should live. We should try to do what Jesus did in every life situation. When it came to God's Word, Jesus held it dearly. Jesus had studied Scripture closely, and He put all authority in it. He was eternally serious about God's Word.

> Don't suppose for a minute that I have come to demolish the Scriptures—either God's Law or the Prophets. I'm not here to demolish but to complete. I am going to put it all together, pull it all together in a vast panorama. God's Law is more real and lasting than the stars in the sky and the ground at your feet. Long after stars burn out and earth wears out, God's Law will be alive and working. (Matthew 5:17-18, MSG)

Jesus couldn't have been more serious about the authority and credibility of God's Word.

He also said, "'I told you that everything written about me in the law of Moses and the prophets and in the Psalms must be fulfilled.' Then he opened their minds to understand the Scriptures" (Luke 24:44-45). I like how that verse talks about Jesus opening their minds to understand the Scriptures.

And the great thing is that He wasn't limited to only opening the minds back then. He continues teaching and opening our minds today. The discipleship continues to you and me!

I encourage you to ask Him to open your mind and heart to what He wants to tell you in His Word. Today and every day.

* * *

Don't Forget (A Recap)

Never utter the words "I'm not much of a reader." Even if it's true, don't say that. (And try not to be that guy.) Read.

Don't be intimidated. Start today. Go to OneYearBibleOnline.com for a printable reading guide. There are also several study Bibles designed to accomplish a complete read-through in a year. No matter how you do it, you'll be glad you did and those around you will be glad you did.

Remember the five basic themes of the Bible. They simplify the idea that it's too huge to understand.

1. The character of God (who he is)

2. Judgment for sin

3. Blessing for faith and obedience

4. Jesus as Lord and Savior and sacrifice for sin

5. The coming kingdom and glory (heaven)

Not feeling so great lately? A little wobbly? Are things just a bit *off*? *Check your foundation.* Are you in God's Word? Why not join a Bible-study group?

Stressed out? Do like Jesus and rely on God's Word for comfort and advice.

Tempted? Do like Jesus and fire off the Word. Memorize passages that are important to you.

It's not only a history book. It's a *now* book. (See 1 Thessalonians 2:13.)

The Bible is 100 percent true. Every word. Second Peter 1:16 says, "For we were not making up clever stories when we told you about the powerful coming of our Lord Jesus Christ. We saw his majestic splendor with our own eyes." (See also 2 Timothy 3:16.)

Jesus was, and is, so very serious about God's Word. We should be too.

The Bible is eternally solid. It's perfectly airtight.

Understand that it is God speaking to you.

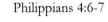

So . . . Who'd Like to Say Grace?

Don't worry about anything; instead, pray about
everything. Tell God what you need, and thank him for all
he has done. Then you will experience God's peace, which
exceeds anything we can understand. His peace will guard
your hearts and minds as you live in Christ Jesus.

Philippians 4:6-7

I mentioned in the last chapter that if you would just start
reading the Bible, I wouldn't care if you tossed this little book
away and got nothing else from *Dashboard Jesus*. That's still what
I'd call the first order of business, but pretty soon after you

started reading the bible, I would have to ask, "So . . . how's
your prayer life?"

It's so elementary really—*Bible reading and prayer*. It's what I was taught as a child. It's what I have known to be true my whole life—that every Christian should read the Bible and pray. But I know firsthand how these essentials can get pushed aside and crowded out of my life.

I encourage you to talk to God. Really talk. And to listen to God. Really listen. That's what prayer is, talking and listening to God. And it's a powerful act. More powerful than we might ever fully know. We've got to understand that prayer makes a difference in the lives of those praying and those being prayed for. I'll say it again: Prayer is powerful. As the seventeenth-century monk Brother Lawrence wrote in his classic "The Practice of the Presence of God," "There is not in the world a kind of life more sweet and delightful than that of a continual conversation with God." And we achieve such a life through prayer.

But sadly, prayer is such an underused blessing. As you read this chapter, try to see what an amazing experience the very act of prayer is for us to participate in. Then grasp the truth that prayer is absolutely vital for your life.

Same Ol' Same Ol'

The Bible tells us two things that could be mistakenly viewed as conflicting and opposite commands regarding prayer. It clearly tells us to pray without ceasing (see 1 Thessalonians 5:17). But on the other hand, Jesus told us not to babble on with long-winded prayers (see Matthew 6:7). *Hmmm* . . . so we wonder, *Am I to be praying continuously or am I to just pray little short prayers?*

Here's what God is telling me about this: "Clay, talk to Me all the time. Really be honest and tell Me everything. But, man, don't bore Me."

Now, I can hear people disputing such a thought. They might think it sounds harsh, coming from God. Some may think that God would never say such a thing and that we couldn't ever possibly bore Him. Think again.

Do you pray? Let me put it another way. Do you talk to God? And do you listen to Him? I'm not talking a cursory prayer before meals. I'm talking about real talk. About anything at all. At any time at all. For any reason at all. Or for no reason sometimes. Kind of how you talk to an old friend, someone you have known a long time and are very comfortable around.

With that friend, you talk about funny things that make you both laugh. And at other times you may bring up more serious matters. Either way, you know this guy is your friend and will always be there for you. Every time. That's what friends do. They just talk. They are comfortable around each other. *Comfortable* and *confident*.

Ephesians 3:12 tells us that "in him and through faith in him we may approach God with *freedom* and *confidence*" (NIV). I like that we can talk to God with freedom and confidence. What if it were the other way around? What if instead of comfortable and confident, talking to God was restrictive and awkward? What if He was standoffish? What if His schedule was full, and He had to pencil you in for next month? Or if you got the feeling that He didn't really want to be around you? We've all known people like that. They are hard to talk to. Hard to get to know. There's just a weird vibe whenever you try to talk to them.

But God has made Himself approachable. Easy to talk to. It is His desire that we come to Him early and often. He wants us seeking Him all the time. Talking to Him. Listening to Him. And He wants *all* our thoughts. He welcomes every variety of topic and life situation. Just like a friend, He wants free and interesting talk. Not boring repetition.

A Reminder: We should pray to God as if He is our best friend. Because He is.

Still think there's no way to bore God? Look at it this way. Imagine going to work one day, and some guy walks up to you and says, "Hey, you're doing a great job! Thanks for the hard work." You'd be flattered. You would think, "What a nice guy!"

Then imagine the next day that same guy comes by and

says, "Hey, you're doing a great job! Thanks for the hard work." You might blink and think to yourself, *Wow, this is the nicest co-worker I have ever met! He must really like me.*

The next day he walks in and says it again: "Hey, you're doing a great job! Thanks for the hard work."

And the next day.

And the next day.

And the next day . . . it's the same thing: "Hey, you're doing a great job! Thanks for the hard work."

Imagine hearing those same words day after day. The - same - exact - words. Kind of weird, wouldn't you say? Then the days turn into weeks, the weeks turn into months, and so on. And every day this guy spouts out those same words: "Hey, you're doing a great job! Thanks for the hard work."

Somewhere in this process you would come to the conclusion that, either:

a. This guy is a robot.

b. I'm in *The Twilight Zone.*

c. This co-worker is mildly insane.

d. He doesn't really care about me all *that much.*

Wouldn't you find it strange if this happened to you? Wouldn't you question how good your relationship really is with this guy?

So think about this . . . what if a man's one prayer to God every day is *Lord, thank You for this day. Forgive us our sins. Use this meal for the nourishment of our bodies. Amen.*

Hmmm, that's nice and all. After all, it is giving thanks. And it is asking for forgiveness. Hear me on this; I'm not slamming such a prayer. We should say these things each day. What I'm getting at here is the idea that so many times our prayers are the same. The exact same words every day. Nothing new. No variety. Nothing funny. Nothing strange. No regular-life talk. Nothing sad. Nothing happy. Nothing exciting. No updates on the latest news. Nothing of concern. Nothing to celebrate. No new questions. Nothing. Just the same ol' same ol'. Just *Lord, thank You for this day. Forgive us our sins. Use this meal for the nourishment of our bodies. Amen.*

Then the next day it's *Lord, thank You for this day. Forgive us our sins. Use this meal for the nourishment of our bodies. Amen.*

Then the next day: *Lord, thank You for this day. Forgive us our sins. Use this meal for the nourishment of our bodies. Amen.*

Day after day . . . it's pretty much that.

I wonder what God thinks when He hears the same twenty words every day from one of His children. From a friend. The same twenty words. With very slight variation. The same exact words.

Or maybe it's this, *Forgive me of my sins and bless me.*

And the next day, *Forgive me of my sins and bless me.*

And the next day, *Forgive me of my sins and bless me.*

I'll say it again; there's not one thing wrong with this prayer. In fact, there's everything right about it. It's perfectly solid, and I darn well better be asking for forgiveness and blessing every day. I'm not condemning this prayer or any prayer for that matter. I'm simply suggesting that we open it up a little. Let's not be quite so predictable. Let's mix it up a bit. Let's make Him laugh. Let's show Him that we want to talk to Him about everything. All the time.

I want God to know that I desire to talk to and listen to Him. I want Him to know that He is more than interesting to me. I want Him to know that He amazes me and that I am captivated by Him. That I want to talk and talk and talk to Him. I want Him to see that's how into Him I am.

The last thing I want God to say is, "It's sad. Clay pretty much says the same exact words to me every day. He talks to Me like he's a robot. Like *I'm* a robot. And I created him to be so much more."

Ephesians 6:18 tells us, "Pray in the Spirit on all occasions with *all kinds* of prayers and requests" (NIV). *All kinds* means *all kinds.* Not same ol' same ol'. C'mon . . . mix it up in there! Relax a little. Talk!

What *Exactly* Do You Mean?

God is all about specifics. It's interesting that even though He knows everything and created everything, He still wants to hear everything from us. So we need to get downright specific with Him with our requests and our thanks. Let's lay it out there for Him. He wants the specifics of our lives. He's interested. He's concerned. He cares. As I read through the Bible, I find more and more examples of how specific God is. Measurements. Lengths of time. Specifications for offerings. Directions on building the temple. Spot-on prophesies. Genealogies. God was and is specific.

In place of praying, *Lord, bless me today*, I am finding that it's better to pray something like this: *Lord, bless me today as I try to write this song. You know I'm stuck on that second verse. Will you help me with that, Lord? I'm ready to finish this song or throw it in the garbage!* Or instead of praying, *Lord, thank You for Your blessings*, a better statement to Him might be, *Lord, what a blessing that was when You helped my daughter get over the flu. She's feeling much better now. Thanks!*

Think of it this way. Imagine parents leaving their kids with a babysitter. They probably wouldn't simply say, "All right, here are our kids. Have fun!" No, a good parent would likely say something like "The kids need to be in bed by nine, and they need to have finished all their homework first. And no television until the homework's done! They can have a snack before bedtime, but be sure they brush their teeth. You can reach us at this number if there's any problem. Any questions?" That's pretty specific. And we should be just as specific when we pray.

Charles Haddon Spurgeon said this about the specifics of our talks with God: "There is a general kind of praying which fails for lack of precision. It is as if a regiment of soldiers should all fire off their guns anywhere. Possibly somebody would be killed, but the majority of the enemy would be missed."[ix]

* * *

A Reminder:

Prayer is most powerful when it's specific. Tell God what's on your mind. Ask God for what you need!

Go ahead; when you pray, tell Him everything. Tell Him exactly what's on your mind. Tell Him exactly what's got you mad or what's got you glad. Don't hold back. Earlier I mentioned the possibility of boring God. Please understand: If your heart is in it (and you aren't acting like some pre-programmed robot), He won't get bored with your words. He will feel loved and engaged. He will listen, and He will get involved. As James told us, "The earnest prayer of a righteous person has great power and produces wonderful results" (5:16).

Walgreens . . . A Holy Place?

Have you ever felt embarrassed to pray somewhere in public? I'm not talking about at church. I'm talking about closing your eyes and praying at McDonald's or Wal-Mart or the post office or any other public place. I've got to admit, there were times when I was seated with a group at a restaurant and wanted the person praying to hurry up and finish his prayer. Or if I was the one praying, I would be overly conscious of onlookers and rush through my prayer. I wonder, *why on earth would I ever feel that way?* Was I so hungry that I just couldn't wait to start eating? I don't think so. I think it's something else. The honest answer hurts me to admit, but I've got to say it. In those uncomfortable moments, I must have been ashamed to be seen as a Christian. At those times, I didn't want to be seen praying. It's as simple and as sad as that.

In the years since my rededication in 1998, my feelings about praying (and praying in public) have come a long way (thank You, God!). Praying is such a blessing, and I have felt the power that comes from both praying alone and praying with others.

One time prior to my recommitment in 1998, I bumped into a longtime friend, Jim Fox, in front of a Walgreens here in Memphis. We talked for a bit, and as we were about to part ways, Jim said, "Hey, man, let's pray." I said, "Sure," but on the inside I was thinking, *P-P-Pray? Right here? In front of Walgreens?* Jim put his hand on my shoulder and began to pray *out loud*. I've got to tell you, it was a little weird for me. I could hear people walking in and out of the store from where we were standing. I wondered what they were thinking. In spite of my discomfort, I closed my eyes and tried to pray with Jim.

Wow, that moment was powerful for me. It was right before my life got back on track with God. It was one of several moments at the time that screamed, "Hey, Clay, *this* is what it's all about!" Yes, it definitely felt strange praying in front of Walgreens, but now I look back and am very thankful that Jim did that. In that moment, Walgreens was a holy place! I began to discover the power that Jesus was talking about when He said, "If two of you agree here on earth concerning anything you ask, my Father in heaven will do it for you. For where two or three gather together as my followers, I am there among them" (Matthew 18:19-20).

I encourage you not to be ashamed to pray in public. But hear me on this; there is a fine line with this. Praying in public is not so that you can be seen and heard praying. It's not about putting on a show. It's just about letting God (and others, too) know that you are comfortable talking to Him, wherever you happen to find yourself. Not being overbearing, but not being ashamed.

Praying . . . It's the *Most* You Can Do

We've all heard it said in times of despair, "It's out of our hands now. All we can do is pray." This is usually said as a last resort, as if prayer is the last and least option in such a time. As if the situation was *ever* in our hands.

How wrong this thinking is! Prayer is the first, best, and constantly appropriate option. Not a last resort. Not a last gasp. Not a fleeting hope. But a regular thought and utterance. Before a crisis. During a crisis. And after the crisis. Before a season of peace. During a season of peace. After a season of peace.

The account of Peter's imprisonment in Acts 12 is a beautiful picture of friends praying in crisis mode for a friend. Peter was in prison with a likely execution coming. His Christian friends must have been very worried. After all, James had just been killed (the first apostle to be martyred), and it was looking as if Peter would be the next to go. Then maybe them.

What did Peter's friends do for him in this time of desperation? Did they send a petition around? Did they organize a rally? Did they write letters? Did they boycott? No.

Did they give up and just admit that there was nothing they could do? Did they just accept that Herod could not be overcome? Did they admit defeat? No.

Peter's friends did something else. In short, they simply did what Christians are supposed to do. They did what was obvious and what was right. They prayed to their Father in heaven.

The result of his friends' prayers was a miracle. There Peter was in prison, with two guards literally chained to him and two more watching the door. (That's a pretty solid guard-to-prisoner ratio.) Herod was finding that when he killed Christians, he earned brownie points with the Jewish leaders. Politically speaking, he liked this. Basically, Peter was a sitting target, about to get popped.

Suddenly, in came an angel who tapped Peter on the side, saying, "Hurry up, man; we're leaving here!" Peter found himself out on the street, a free man. Still reeling from the experience, he naturally went to see his friends. When he got to the house, the girl who answered the door was so freaked out when she heard his voice that she didn't even let him come inside. In shock, she ran back in to tell the others. They all thought she had lost her mind until they went outside. And there he was. They were amazed.

God heard their faithful prayers, and He did something remarkable. It's as simple as that. The psalmist sang,

O my people, trust in him at all times.

Pour out your heart to him,

for God is our refuge. (62:8)

A Reminder: Prayer should be your first resort—not the last.

What a biblically solid and Christian act it is to pray *for someone else*. I enjoyed a sermon once by Dr. Gary Chapman at his church in North Carolina. His topic that day was prayer (specifically, *praying for others*). I'll never forget what he told us. He said,

> If you ever get the urge to pray for someone, do it. It's not some wrong or misdirected feeling you are having. Satan will never urge you to pray for someone. It's God urging you. As you go throughout your day, pray for a co-worker. Pray for the custodian. Pray for your boss.

Students, pray for your teachers. Teacher, pray for your students. At the grocery, pray for the cashier. Pray for the postal worker. Pray for anyone at all. Begin to intentionally look for others to pray for.[x]

Then Dr. Chapman took it a step further, saying, "And pray for the drug dealers in your city. Pray for the local prostitutes, too." I wanted to jump out of my chair and say, "Yes! Yes! Yes! You go, Gary!" You just don't hear that kind of challenge from the pulpit very often. It was so much like Christ to suggest such a thing. As Christian men, our goal is to become more like Christ, so let's get outside ourselves and pray for others.

Monday Night Football

I thought if I titled this section "The Utmost Importance of Fasting," a lot of guys would skip over it, so I went with something that's near and dear to most of us. I mean, what's better than Monday night football? I remember as a kid not being allowed to watch the second half of Monday night games because it was after my bedtime for a school night. Man, that hurt . . . missing the whole second half! That's probably what's wrong with me today. But I digress.

So, this section *is* about fasting, (not football, sorry.) We often hear the word *prayer* teamed with the word *fasting*. There is a good reason for that. They go hand in hand. Fasting is an agent to help us see and hear God more clearly. Just like prayer, fasting is about shutting out distractions in order to seek God. When we put food aside for a while, our bodies naturally call out for it. The method in fasting is to call out to God as our bodies call out for food. The results are undeniable.

J. R. Mahon from XXXchurch.com wrote honestly about his experience of going without food in an effort to hear from God. "I would love to tell you it was the greatest thing I have ever done besides marrying my wife. I can and it was. . . . It throws you into the presence of God. No waiting room. Immediate access to the Creator of the world. It was amazing."[xi]

I hope that J. R.'s enthusiasm will make some guys want to start fasting, but I'm sure in most cases it won't. Why? It's simple . . . food just tastes too good. People like it too much to consider ever putting it aside for a day or two. (Oh, I didn't mention that J. R. was writing about his *forty-day* fast!) Yeah, food is wonderful, and we'd rather not stop enjoying it. Not to mention those pesky side effects that accompany a fast: hunger pangs, weakness. Who wants that?

I understand not really wanting to fast because I enjoy food about as much as anyone. Every time I see a cinnamon-raisin bun in the window of Au Bon Pain on one of my many strolls through the Atlanta Airport, I hear a little voice. It's the sweet roll talking to me. "Hey, Clay, I know you had breakfast in Memphis, but wouldn't you like me too?" Outback's Aussie cheese fries are a favorite of mine also. And nachos of any kind. And Slim Jims. And mint-chocolate ice cream. And . . .

and . . . and . . . You get the picture. I like to eat. But here's what God is telling me: "Clay, I get it. Food is good. But you need *Me* more."

That's essentially what Jesus was saying when Satan tempted Him to eat during His fast in the desert. Jesus said, "People do not live by bread alone, but by every word that comes from the mouth of God" (Matthew 4:4). Jesus spoke of fasting again in Matthew 6.

> And when you fast, don't make it obvious, as the hypocrites do, for they try to look miserable and disheveled so people will admire them for their fasting. I tell you the truth, that is the only reward they will ever get. But when you fast, comb your hair and wash your face. Then no one will notice that you are fasting, except your Father, who knows what you do in private. And your Father, who sees everything, will reward you. (verses 16-18)

As much as I'd like to believe that fasting is for some people but not for others (so maybe it's not for me!), I can't rewrite or deny what Jesus said there. He said, "*When* you fast . . ." Not "*If* you fast . . ." or "*If you feel called* to fast . . ." Nope. He said, "*When* you fast . . ."

This all stems from how much Jesus loves me. A lot. A ton! And He wants to be close to me. But sadly I let Him get crowded out sometimes. Fasting is a way to say to Jesus, *I love You, too, and I want to be with You and hear from You. As I deny my hunger, Lord, I ask You to be with me closer than ever. Speak to me. Fill me.* Talk about a powerful prayer! That one won't bore God. That's the kind of prayer He runs to.

* * *

A Reminder: Fasting is a way to focus your attention where it needs to be. It's another way to say, *What do You have for me today, Lord?*

I challenge you to begin some kind of fast. I've heard of people fasting from things other than food. Music, TV, golf, Monday Night Football (ouch). Hey, whatever it takes to quit something for a while and get closer to God. And I'm not talking about forty days. Try *one* day. Believe me, you will feel it. And as your heart is pointed to God, He will speak clearly to you. Here's a simple fast that sets aside all food for twenty-four hours.

The Yom Kippur Fast[xii]

Start by skipping your evening meal.

The next day, skip breakfast and lunch.

Wait until after sundown to eat again.

Done! That's the Yom Kippur fast. "Yom Kippur? I'm not Jewish," you might say, (if you're not Jewish). Hey, listen . . . Jesus was Jewish; it's not exactly a bad thing. Spend the time that you would have spent preparing (or driving to) and eating those meals in prayer. Make the whole experience an effort to get more of God.

Jesus fasted, and He tells us to do the same. It's not some test to show how close to God you are. It's the effort to get closer to Him.

It's Okay, God . . . I'm Good Here

Many times, *not* praying is our way of saying, "It's okay, God . . . I'm good here." That might sound extreme, but really, what else are we communicating when we fail to pray? In those times we must feel that we can handle things on our own. And we might be a tad overconfident. We tend to fall into thinking, *This life rests on my shoulders,* instead of admitting, *Lord, I can't bear this alone. In fact, I need You to carry me.* Instead of putting things in His hands, we try to go it alone. *After all,* we think, *I'm a grown man. I can handle this!*

In Mark 9:14-29, the disciples found themselves in a situation where they had to admit they couldn't do something. They were shocked when they were unable to cast out an evil spirit. They had been performing miracles and were used to the process, but this time they just couldn't pull it off. Understand what I just said: "*They* just couldn't pull it off."

Perhaps they had become too sure of themselves. Maybe seeing miracle after miracle was getting routine. Their overconfidence finally led them to failure. When Jesus showed up, He commented sadly on the overall lack of faith He was seeing. He then commanded the evil spirit to leave the boy. And, of course, it did.

Afterward, the disciples asked Jesus why they were unable to drive out the evil spirit. They were confused at their failure to deliver. Jesus simply told them, "This kind can come out by nothing but prayer and fasting" (Mark 9:29, NKJV).

Jesus was basically telling His guys that they were getting too sure of themselves and had been slacking off on constantly seeking God's hand on their every act. It was His friendly reminder for them not to lose their focus and never to forget where their true source of power came from.

But His reminder wasn't just for the disciples. It's for us, too. I need to be reminded as well. With every activity that I jump into, I need to be saying, *Lord, go with me on this* or *Lord, stop me now if You're not into this.*

* * *

A Reminder: Seek God's advice on everything you do. Prayer will keep you in touch with what God wants for your life.

Don't Just Take My Word for It

Here are some thoughts on prayer from men and women I consider giants of our faith. They lived so close to God that I just shake my head and marvel at their selflessness, their sacrifices, and their hearts for service. And they all agreed that prayer is paramount, that prayer is needed, and that prayer is a blessing.

> "Prayer does not fit us for the greater work; prayer *is* the greater work." -Oswald Chambers

> "When a Christian shuns fellowship with other

Christians, the devil smiles. When he stops studying the Bible, the devil laughs. When he stops praying, the devil shouts for joy."
-Corrie ten Boom

"God shapes the world by prayer. The more praying there is in the world, the better the world will be, the mightier the forces against evil." -E. M. Bounds

"Work, work, from morning until late at night. In fact, I have so much to do that I shall have to spend the first three hours in prayer."
-Martin Luther

"To desire revival, and at the same time neglect prayer and devotion is to wish one way and walk another." -A. W. Tozer

"The one concern of the devil is to keep Christians from praying. He fears nothing from prayerless studies, prayerless work, and prayerless religion. He laughs at our toil, mocks at our wisdom, but trembles when we pray."
-Samuel Chadwick

* * *

Hush, Y'all . . . I'm Doing My Daily Detox

So much of what prayer is all about comes down to one thing: focus. When we pray, we put our focus on God. On what He wants. On what He is saying. The cool part about having this sharp focus on Him is that you don't have to close your eyes and stop what you are doing. You can be at home working on your lawn or at your job or at a ball game or at the mall or wherever. Prayer is just as powerful while you are on the go as when you are in some chapel or quiet place.

At the same time, though, we should definitely look for those still, undisturbed, and totally focused moments alone with God. I get so overloaded with constant media, images, sights, sounds, and activities that at some point every day I have to say, "Hold on! I've got to detox from all this. My brain is about to explode!" That's precisely when a quiet time is so refreshing and necessary.

A lot of men find this very hard to do. They're busy with jobs or family activities, and they just can't squeeze in a quiet time. If this is you, let me make a suggestion. Try doing this as you go to sleep. Think about it . . . it's not like you will have to carve out that time. You end up there every day without fail. So why not empty yourself of the day's onslaught and talk to God at the end of each day? Right there in bed, quietly focus and talk and listen to God. What better way to close out each day? There *is* no better way.

I encourage you to take a little time each day to turn off everything but your focus on God. I've suggested nighttime, but really it could be anytime. Morning, afternoon, or night—it doesn't really matter. Depending on your schedule, any time can be perfect when it comes to getting quiet with God. C. S. Lewis opted for a morning quiet time. I like how he put it.

"It comes the very moment you wake up each morning. All your wishes and hopes for the day rush at you like wild animals. And the first job each morning consists simply in shoving them all back; in listening to that other voice, taking that other point of view, letting that other larger, stronger, quieter life come flowing in. And so on, all day. Standing back from all your natural fussings and frettings; coming in out of the wind."[xiii]

Simply being quiet has become a lost art form in today's world. So many people must have a television or radio going at all times or they just can't function. This is sad.

I encourage you to be quiet. "Hush, y'all," they say down here in the South. Seriously, empty yourself of everything and listen to God. And talk too. Just you and Him. Every day.

Don't Forget (A Recap)

Be free and confident in your talks with God. Mix it up a little. Don't bore Him with the same ol' same ol'. He didn't create a robot. He created you. And He wants to hear from you!

Get specific with Him. This *won't* bore Him. He wants to hear it.

Praying in public: Don't show off, but don't deny it either. Just pray.

Satan doesn't give us the urge to pray for anyone, ever. But God does. So pray for your friends in times of need. And pray for strangers you see out in public. And for that matter, pray for anyone at all who comes to mind.

Take up fasting, and you will hear from God. Jesus did it and told us to do it. Your stomach will be empty for a moment, but you will be filling up!

Take everything to God. Don't ever assume, "It's okay, God . . . I'm good here." Because truthfully, without Him, we are *never* "good here."

Do a daily detox. Clear your mind. Get quiet with God.

* * *

Clay Crosse

I'm Just a Workin' Man

What do people really get for all their hard work? I have seen the burden God has placed on us all . . . So I concluded there is nothing better than to be happy and enjoy ourselves as long as we can. And people should eat and drink and enjoy the fruits of their labor, for these are gifts from God.

Ecclesiastes 3:9-10, 12-13

Does your job ever get you down? If so, you're not alone. It's a common feeling. In fact, it can be that way for everyone from time to time. While it's a blessing to be employed, in some ways work can also be a curse. Yes, we are blessed to have our jobs—no doubt about it. But sometimes work can really be a pain. (As Bruce Springsteen sang, "End of the day, factory whistle cries / Men walk through these gates with death in their eyes."[xiv])

A Blessing and a Curse

Let's be honest here; sometimes it takes all you can do to get in your car and head off to work. Some co-workers just rub you the wrong way. Some drive you crazy and make you want to scream. At times you think, *I'd really love my job if it weren't for all these . . . people.* And certain bosses are not so fun to be around either. Many workers remark about their boss, "This guy's no smarter or more qualified than I am. Why is *he* the boss?" The work itself can be redundant too. What a drag. We've all asked the question, "How many more days until the weekend?"

Why is work so hard sometimes? Well, it would be easy to deduce that work takes effort and that effort is difficult. Really, though, it's not that simple. Truth is, work was originally created to be a complete joy. But something changed.

I suppose we could blame the whole thing on Adam and Eve. Why Adam and Eve? Well, let's look back. We all know their story, how they were the first to sin. Ah, sin . . . the very thing that has caused anything bad for the rest of us throughout history started with Adam and Eve. Thanks a lot, you two. We all appreciate it.

But we can't really hang it on them, can we? If it had been me, the outcome would have been the same. And, yes, you too would have eventually sinned at some point to start the whole ball rolling.

God showed immediately that with sin, there must be consequences. What kind of consequences? Along with God's curses on the snake and then on Eve and all women to follow (see Genesis 3:14-16), God pronounced a curse on Adam and all mankind that would follow him. (This is where the story affects your work and how it can be difficult.) In essence, the curse stated that all work from that point on would be, for lack of a better word, *hard*. Really hard. With many obstacles and challenges (see Genesis 3:17-19). On top of the hard-work part of the curse, it also contained this little side note: At the end of all your backbreaking hard work, you'll die. *Nice.*

* * *

Obstacles and challenges at work. Sound familiar? We are simply feeling the effects of that curse from long ago. But, hey, enough with the negative. Let's go back to the *blessing* part I mentioned.

Work . . . what a blessing! And what an honor to be given that blessing in the form of a job. Notice how Solomon talked about work. Ecclesiastes is one of the more misunderstood books in the Bible. I myself have read that book and thought, *What a little whiner that Solomon became!* But the more we dig, the more we see the true message of his rants. A message of our total dependence on God and the blessings that result.

What do people really get for all their hard

work? I have seen the burden God has placed on us all . . . So I concluded there is nothing better than to be happy and enjoy ourselves as long as we can. And people should eat and drink and enjoy the fruits of their labor, for these are gifts from God. (Ecclesiastes 3:9-10, 12-13)

Hmmm, this makes me think that God's curse on Adam is, in a roundabout way, *a gift!* Verse 11 sheds some light on this mystery: "God has made everything beautiful for its own time. He has planted eternity in the human heart, but even so, people cannot see the whole scope of God's work from beginning to end."

As a Christian man in the workforce, you've got to try to understand that last part there: "People cannot see the whole scope of God's work from beginning to end." We must cling to this on days we are confused, frustrated, and generally hacked off at work. We must understand that God is there with us and that He is blessing us. Sometimes God is certainly a mystery, and our current situation can be mysteriously tough. But one thing is never a mystery—*whether or not He loves us.* We should never have to ask, "Does God love me today?" We may wonder what the heck is going on with certain situations in our lives, but we should never doubt His love throughout those challenges. This is especially comforting to know when you're at work. Yep, work is hard. But God is blessing you through the hard work.

* * *

A Reminder: God's ways can be mysterious and confusing sometimes, but we should never doubt His love for us.

Meet Your New Boss

In my years of working various jobs, I have had some amazing bosses. Sharp, focused, honest, and caring. Some of them were the hands-on type, rolling up their sleeves and jumping in on most every project. Others weren't so directly involved day in and day out; they were better at delegating and assigning the right task to the right person. Regardless of their styles, the bottom line was this: These bosses were great leaders. The kind of men and women who made me want to work hard for them and always give my best.

Yes, I've had some great bosses, but I've got to admit that a few of my supervisors weren't so wonderful. Distracted, unfair, unclear, unhappy, and generally unpleasant to be around. Truthfully, I looked at some of them and had to ask, "How in the world did they even become a boss?" I wasn't all that motivated to give those bosses *nearly* my best.

Let me tell you—this kind of thinking was flat-out wrong. I should have never let the quality of my work be determined by how much I liked my boss. It's not for me to determine whether or not my boss is worthy of my best.

In Colossians 3:22-24, Paul slammed home this truth as clearly as possible:

"Slaves, obey your earthly masters in everything you do. Try to please them all the time, not just when they are watching you. Serve them sincerely because of your reverent fear of the Lord. Work willingly at whatever you do, as though you were working for the Lord rather than for people. Remember that the Lord will give you an inheritance as your reward, and that the Master you are serving is Christ."

Keep in mind that in Paul's day, slaves made up most of the workforce. Rather than using terms like *employee* and *employer*, they just called them slaves and masters.

As this scripture starts to soak in, imagine that you have a new boss—because you do. If you don't care much for your boss, this should come as good news. But if you like your boss a lot, you may be thinking, *I don't want a new boss. I like my boss.* Trust me here. This new boss is better. God is your boss. Get comfortable with this truth. It's a good thing.

As Christian men, we should commit to always work hard, for no other reason than because we love God and want to obey Him. He's our boss, and our work is for Him.

A Reminder:

God is your ultimate boss. Do you work as if your next raise is up to Him. Actually, it is.

The tough thing is that we still have to show up every workday and face that man or woman who happens to be our earthly boss. And what if that boss is difficult? What if you know firsthand that your boss has been dishonest and unfair? What if doing a good job for a bad person feels like you are supporting evil in some way? That may sound extreme, but there are Christian workers out there who feel that way and who are very conflicted just showing up to work for their bosses. To those people I would say that there's nothing wrong with keeping your antennae up for a different job situation somewhere else. But as long as you are under that boss, you are commanded to give 100 percent.

Buckle your seat belt before you read this next bit from the apostle Peter.

> "You who are servants, be good servants to your masters—not just to good masters, but also to bad ones. What counts is that you put up with it for God's sake when you're treated badly for no good reason. There's no particular virtue in accepting punishment that you well deserve. But if you're treated badly for good behavior and continue in spite of it to be a good servant, that is what counts with God.
>
> This is the kind of life you've been invited into, the kind of life Christ lived. He suffered everything that came his way so you would know that it could be done, and also know how to do it, step-by-step.
>
> He never did one thing wrong,
>
> Not once said anything amiss.
>
> They called him every name in the book and he said nothing back. He suffered in silence,

content to let God set things right. He used his servant body to carry our sins to the Cross so we could be rid of sin, free to live the right way. His wounds became your healing. You were lost sheep with no idea who you were or where you were going. Now you're named and kept for good by the Shepherd of your souls." (1 Peter 2:18-25, MSG)

Wow. This is a slam-dunk passage in which Peter compared our little sufferings in the workplace to Christ's suffering on the cross. He rightly placed Jesus as our only standard when we feel mistreated. This is a strong challenge that should make us say, "Amazing! If Jesus endured *that*, then I can endure *this*."

* * *

God Provides Your Skill Set

One of the coolest aspects of God being your boss is that He not only gives you specific tasks to perform, but He also gives you specific abilities to do them well. That's right. He gives you the skills you need to do whatever work He gives you. He won't just say, "Do this," and then leave you high and dry. That's not how He leads. That's not His management style.

Let's look at a worker in the Bible named Bezalel. God touched this guy in a specific way for a specific task.

Then the LORD said to Moses, "Look, I have specifically chosen Bezalel son of Uri, grandson of Hur, of the tribe of Judah. I have filled him with the Spirit of God, giving him great wisdom, ability, and expertise in all kinds of crafts. He is a master craftsman, expert in working with gold, silver, and bronze. He is skilled in engraving and mounting gemstones and in carving wood. He is a master at every craft!" (Exodus 31:1-5)

It's interesting to note that this is the first mention in Scripture of someone being filled with the Spirit of God. That phrase "filled with the Spirit" conjures up all kinds of thoughts with some people. We hear "filled with the Spirit" and imagine things like speaking in tongues, lifting of hands, or an energetic/enthusiastic music style during worship. We have limited "it" (The Holy Spirit) to those things.

But here God filled Bezalel with His Spirit so that he would be a great worker. No doubt about it; his job was very important. After all, he was building God's holy tabernacle. This is a clear picture of how God fills us to do important work. It's His Spirit that makes a Christian wise and productive in the workplace. (And we thought it was a college degree and experience!)

Not only did God get involved with such paramount tasks as building the tabernacle, He jumps in on our normal—not so paramount—jobs. Jobs like driving a bus, selling insurance, teaching tenth-grade geometry, flying an aircraft, filling a cavity, hosting a radio show, cleaning an office building, delivering pizzas, building houses, replacing transmissions, preparing a vanilla latte, and every other job out there. God cares about all of our work. He cares about every aspect of our lives. He wants to be in the center of it all, and He wants us to be great at all of it. What a boss!

Check out how God got involved with a typical profession, one that might have been perceived as a little lower and less cool on the job chain than building God's temple—farming.

Give me your closest attention.

Do farmers plow and plow and do nothing but plow?

Or harrow and harrow and do nothing but harrow?

After they've prepared the ground, don't they plant?

Don't they scatter dill and spread cumin,

Plant wheat and barley in the fields

and raspberries along the borders?

They know exactly what to do and when to do it.

Their God is their teacher.

And at the harvest, the delicate herbs and spices,

the dill and cumin, are treated delicately.

On the other hand, wheat is threshed and milled, but still not endlessly.

The farmer knows how to treat each kind of grain.

He's learned it all from GOD-*of-the-Angel-Armies* [The Lord of Hosts],

who knows everything about when and how and where. (Isaiah 28:23-29, MSG,)

Just as God helped Bezalel do grand work and the farmer do common work, God will help you at your job. *Keep visualizing Him as your boss.* The most caring boss. The wisest boss. The perfect boss.

* * *

Paul also gave instructions to employers: "Masters, treat your slaves in the same way. Don't threaten them; remember, you both have the same Master in heaven, and he has no favorites" (Ephesians 6:9).

Christian bosses should understand that they and their employees are both servants of the same Master and should treat them accordingly. They are both children of the same Father—God. These bosses should take great care when it comes to their employees, much like a big brother would protect a little brother or sister. Standing up for them. Watching out for them. Encouraging them. Providing a safe work environment for them. Treating them with dignity and respect. Paying them what they deserve. And handling daily business activity with integrity and honesty.

The Real You Comes Out . . . At Work

Have you noticed how we tend to separate the different areas of our lives into neat little compartments? Boxes, if you will. For example:

> In this box, I will keep my home life. (The time at home with my family.)

> This other box holds my work life. (Time at the workplace or wherever my work takes me.)

> In this box, I keep my church life. (Going to church and any activities involving my church.)

This box is for my free time/leisure time. (Golfing. Going to the movies. Watching sporting events. Working out at the health club.)

The thing about all these different boxes is they can cause us to act a little or a lot differently when we are participating in these various areas of life. We put on one face at church. Then another face at work. At home we relax a little and don't worry as much about our face. Then later on the golf course, it's another face.

That's right. Different faces for different situations. I'd like to say, "No way; I would never change who I am for different situations. I am always the same guy." But the truth is, I know that sometimes I have switched faces to match the specific place I was in. This confession challenges me to be the same man in all areas of life. After all, God doesn't change. And His standards for me don't change. He should be squarely in my focus no matter where I am and what I am doing.

* * *

A Reminder: If you're a different person at work, get reacquainted with your authentic self. And probably with God!

This book is all about reminders; as I've said before, guys just seem to forget how God wants us to act. One place where we really tend to forget who we are and how we are supposed to act is at work. For some reason, many men simply let their guards down and become a different person at work.

Work is where we spend a big percentage of our lives. As Phoenix Seminary professor Wayne Grudem said, "Work provides great opportunities to glorify God, and also presents great temptations to sin."[xv] As a result, who we are at work is in many respects *who we really are.*

As Christians we should take very seriously our

reputations at work. We should routinely ask:

> "What do my co-workers really see in me?"

> "How has my history here, day in and day out, determined my reputation?"

> "Is my word solid here?"

> "Am I trusted?"

> "Do I care about the quality of my work?"

> "Am I a good teammate?"

And married men must ask: "Do my co-workers see me as a faithful husband? Or do they know that I have a wandering eye and that I flirt?"

Honesty at Work

So much of a man's reputation at work centers on one thing: *honesty*. I've heard it said that "there are a hundred ways to steal but only one way to be honest."[xvi] And one of the easiest places to steal seems to be at work. I suppose this is because there is some level of trust among co-workers. They are not strangers; (we see each other every day. In a weird way, it's kind of like family. And who would steal from his own family? Well, we all know that's naïve thinking because stealing at work is very common.

God tells us straight up, "You must not steal" (Exodus 20:15). Never. In any way. From anyone. But what do you think He means? While literal stealing will get you fired, there are endless little dishonest actions which could be considered stealing that might go unnoticed at work. Or do they?

What kind of little dishonest actions? Things like leaving early from work (but still being on the clock). Or fudging on the numbers here and there. Or being dishonest with a client. Or simply being an exaggerator for your own benefit.

Let me tell you something about these so-called little actions. If any of your co-workers have seen you, *they will never forget.* You have built your reputation. If you are reading this and feel bad and want to change your past, you can't. What you can do, though, is go to your co-workers and apologize. It's the only way to regain their trust. *And* you must build a new history of solid ethics. Prove to your co-workers that you have learned from your past and that you want to be better for the team.

I know that sounds like an uncomfortable thing to do, but believe me, by doing this you will gain respect and be appreciated. As a Christian man, you must use God as your example of a trusted and faithful employee and co-worker: "The One who called you is completely dependable. If he said it, he'll do it!" (1 Thessalonians 5:24, MSG).

Decide now who you will be at work. Be a man who honors God every hour he's on the job. If your normal work face hasn't looked much like a follower of Christ, then change it. Be the kind of co-worker you want to be around. Hardworking. Encouraging. Honest. Consistent. Faithful.

Work Is *Worship*

Most people assume that there are Christian jobs and secular jobs. For example,

> Being a missionary—Christian job
>
> Being a pastor—Christian job
>
> Working on an assembly line—secular job
>
> Selling insurance—secular job

The thinking is that while some people do sacred work for God, everyone else just does secular work.

> I've got to tell you—*that's not how God sees it.*

Whatever your job happens to be, your good and faithful work honors God. In fact, work itself should be considered an act of worship to God. Some people limit their times of worship to the music portion of their weekly church service. *That's* when they worship. *Right then.* When will we get it that our whole lives are worship services to God?

A little word study here: God commanded us, "Six days shalt thou labor, and do all thy work" (Exodus 20:9, KJV). The Hebrew word used here for *labor* can also be translated as *serve* or *worship*. From God's perspective, labor, service, and worship are almost synonymous. The word translated as *work* (*mela'kah*) can also mean *ministry*.

So read it this way now: "Six days you shall *worship* and do all your *ministry*." Very, very interesting. This paints a little different picture of work, doesn't it?

* * *

Let me encourage you here. Like I said, I realize that work can be hard, that some co-workers are less than desirable to be around, and that your (earthly) boss may not be the best. Despite these realities, stay focused on your (real) boss—God. Don't allow Him to be crowded out of your life while you are at work. In fact, invite Him along with you every day and worship Him with the work of your hands.

A Reminder:

Doing your best at work honors God.

Wealth—God, You're Okay with That, *Right?*

So much of what work is about seems to always come back to
one thing: money. After all, our jobs are how we make a living.
Our jobs allow us to pay the bills and provide for our families.
And it's how the company (our employer) makes their profit.
Gaining wealth can become the central driving force behind
the whole effort.

And we are great at the comparison game. You know
that game, right? The one where everyone knows what
everyone else makes. Salary comparison. Possession
comparison. It's a pretty ugly sport, and many men seem to
play it, in one way or another.

Know this . . . God is completely fine with a man
having wealth. What He's not so cool with is a man loving that
wealth and desiring it to the point that it is the constant
thought of his life.

And that's the rub. Money cannot be our motivator to
get up and go to work every day. Money cannot be our goal. It
can't be the only reason we work. We need more to motivate
us than just our paycheck. Money must not become our god.
That's precisely what Paul warned us about: "Lust for money
brings trouble and nothing but trouble. Going down that path,
some lose their footing in the faith completely and live to
regret it bitterly ever after" (1 Timothy 6:10, MSG). In short,
have money but don't love money. It's perfectly okay to
acknowledge that a result from our hard work can be wealth. In

fact, it's a gift from God.

In biblical times, God gave the greatest power to attain wealth to Solomon. Seriously, this guy was loaded. However, God didn't just drop gold bars from heaven on Solomon; rather He gave Solomon solid business sense and unequaled wisdom. Even through Solomon's low points and personal failures, this wisdom made him able to rule wisely, judge well, and, along the way, make a huge profit. Doing his work well and being satisfied with it were two central keys to human satisfaction for Solomon.

* * *

A Reminder:

If you're focused on money, you can't possibly be focused on God.

Got My Mind On My Money

Those of us who don't exactly have a cash flow like Solomon look at money in a different way. Frankly, we want more of it, and we worry about not having enough of it. Many men live paycheck to paycheck. Others constantly fret about just paying the bills and providing. We agonize over future expenses like college for the kids, weddings, medical bills, and retirement. We men are some serious worriers.

But Jesus told us over and over again, "Don't worry" (see Matthew 6:25-34). He also reminded us that between God and money, we must choose which we will serve: "You can't worship two gods at once. Loving one god, you'll end up hating the other. Adoration of one feeds contempt for the other. You can't worship God and Money both" (Matthew 6:24, MSG).

We've all heard it said, "Money makes the world go 'round." (God hears that, laughs a little, and thinks, *No, it doesn't. I make the world go 'round.*) But money certainly motivates billions of people. And money calls out to non-Christians and Christians alike. We see a wealthy person, and we think, *Man, I'd like to have his money.* We can't help but think, *Wow, look at that house.* We see a great vacation destination on TV and say, "That would be nice, but we just can't afford it." We tend to think more about what we don't have instead of the blessings we do have. Ultimately, we just think *too much* about money. And we think *too highly* of men in our world who have lots of it.

Picture the CEO of a huge company walking in for a

surprise visit to his lower-level employees' workplace. Everyone freezes, almost bowing in reverence. It's exciting. Of all people, *him*! Coming *here*! People's faces blush as they nod and shake his hand. There's a buzz in the room simply due to his presence.

Someone peeks out the window. "Check out his car. Nice! That thing cost more than my house!" Someone else whispers, "And have you ever seen his house? Whoa! We could all live in that thing and never see each other. It's as big as a hotel."

Rich people are admired. Sought after. Drooled over. Kissed up to. Respected. Others want what they have and wish they could be like them. And for one reason: money.

Don't you know—without me even telling you—that God thinks this is ridiculous? As God's children, with access to eternal riches, we should *never* admire anyone for his money. Never.

Jesus was a master storyteller. His stories and illustrations, known as parables, drove home His points in unforgettable ways. He told a particularly amazing parable about a rich man and a poor man. And remember, Jesus detested the love of money. He warned and warned about its temporary and destructive nature.

Again, buckle up before you read this next bit.

There once was a rich man, expensively dressed in the latest fashions, wasting his days in conspicuous consumption. A poor man named Lazarus, covered with sores, had been dumped on his doorstep. All he lived for was to get a meal from scraps off the rich man's table. His best friends were the dogs who came and licked his sores.

Then he died, this poor man, and was taken up by the angels to the lap of Abraham. The rich man also died and was buried. In hell and in torment, he looked up and saw Abraham in the distance and Lazarus in his lap. He called out, "Father Abraham, mercy! Have mercy! Send Lazarus to dip his finger in water to cool my tongue. I'm in agony in this fire."

But Abraham said, "Child, remember that in your lifetime you got the good things and Lazarus the bad things. It's not like that here. Here he's consoled and you're tormented. Besides, in all these matters there is a huge chasm set between us so that no one can go from us to you even if he wanted to, nor can anyone cross over from you to us."

The rich man said, "Then let me ask you, Father: Send him to the house of my father where I have five brothers, so he can tell them the score and warn them so they won't end up here in this place of torment."

Abraham answered, "They have Moses and the Prophets to tell them the score. Let them listen to them."

"I know, Father Abraham," he said, "but they're not listening. If someone came back to them from the dead, they would change their ways."

Abraham replied, "If they won't listen to Moses and the Prophets, they're not going to be convinced by someone who rises from the dead." (Luke 16:19-31, MSG)

Incredible! This story told by Jesus should really shake up any Christian who even remotely thinks that money is the way. Imagine that wealthy man sitting in hell crying out for poor Lazarus to dip his finger in water and place it on his burning lips. That is just masterful storytelling by Jesus. (The kind of story that I need as I struggle in this materialistic world.)

Seriously! This parable is a straight-up reminder that any rich man who does not know Christ should *not* be admired by any Christian. We should *not* covet his life. We should *not* covet his possessions. He may appear to have it all together, but we know that he's lost. He's sad. To be pitied, not admired. Doomed without Christ. Even with all he has, he's missing what he needs the most.

* * *

A Little Note to the Workaholics

Some men will read what I've written about how hard work is and think, *Hey, work's not a pain for me at all. In fact, I love it! I can't get enough of it. I think about it all the time. I bring it home. I even take it on vacation with me. I love work!*

Well, good for them, *I suppose.* Except for that "I can't get enough" part and the part about taking it on vacation. We need to put our jobs in perspective and realize that they are just a portion of our lives. And not the most important portion, for that matter. Yes, we should be thankful for our jobs and give our best, but they should not dominate our lives.

> This is the case of a man who is all alone, without a child or a brother, yet who works hard to gain as much wealth as he can. But then he asks himself, "Who am I working for? Why am I giving up so much pleasure now?" It is all so meaningless and depressing. (Ecclesiastes 4:8)

"Depressing," Solomon said. Many workaholics struggle with depression. It's like they never have enough. It's just go, go, go. They are much like the hamster on his spinning wheel. Running his legs off but never getting anywhere. Solomon also mentioned that the man has no family. But the rub here is that many workaholics *do have families.* Families that need more of them.

Work is hard enough. Learn to balance it with the joys

of leisure. (I know, most guys reading this won't need much prodding here. Most of us are more than comfortable with a little—or a lot—of R & R. But some do struggle with letting go.) Remember, "One handful of peaceful repose is better than two fistfuls of worried work" (Ecclesiastes 4:6, MSG).

Be the Aroma of Christ at Work

Jesus talked and talked about how we should love our neighbors. And I'm sure He didn't mean just the people who *live* near us. He also meant the people who *work* near us. In the next cubicle. Just down the assembly line. In the classroom across the hall. In the next office. Your business partner. Your co-workers. Your boss.

Not only is work noble and God-ordained, it is an opportunity to reach people for Christ as commanded in the Great Commission. This gives us a whole new perspective on our jobs when we realize that God wants us to actively reach out to those around us while we are working. Truth is, loving others is a much higher purpose for our jobs than making money or advancing our careers. God is not asking, "How much money did you earn this week?" Rather He is asking, "Who did you reach out to this week? Tell Me about that."

* * *

A Reminder:

As Christians, we should be a reflection of Christ no matter where we go— particularly at work.

As Christians, we should be bringing something rare and special into the workplace every day: "Now he uses us to spread the knowledge of Christ everywhere, like a sweet perfume" (2 Corinthians 2:14).

Sweet perfume? And you thought this book was for men. I can just hear some good ol' boy somewhere saying, "Man, don't talk to me about being no sweet perfume at my job. You ain't been to my job. It's *far* from sweet. Those boys down there . . . they're bad news. Ain't nothing sweet about my job."

Understand, by calling it a sweet perfume, Paul was

simply suggesting that we can diffuse Christ wherever we go. As we have admitted, work can be very tough. It can stink. What will it hurt to provide a better "smell" around the jobsite?

Paul went on to say, "Our lives are a Christ-like fragrance rising up to God. But this fragrance is perceived differently by those who are being saved and by those who are perishing" (2 Corinthians 2:15). *Hmmm*, we must be prepared for that last part there. No matter how kind, encouraging, hardworking, honest, and faithful we are at work, there will still be those who just don't like us. The key is for us to stay consistent and focused.

Don't Forget (A Recap)

Be thankful for your job. Even though it's tough sometimes, it's still a tremendous blessing. Thank God for the work.

Know that God is your real boss. Work hard for Him!

Build a solid reputation among your peers at work. Be 100 percent honest, supportive, and reliable.

Actually worship God through normal, everyday labor.

Be thankful for the cash, but don't be a slave to it.

Love others at work. Provide the aroma of Christ.

It might not be a bad idea to put a little Dashboard Jesus (or a scripture) on your desk or near your PC. Just a thought. If not, then for sure have your Bible nearby. It speaks a lot about you to others, and beyond that, you just need it close by. Reminders . . . we've got to have them. Especially at work.

* * *

Who, Me? Do That?

My dear children, let's not just talk about love;

let's practice real love.

1 John 3:18, MSG

Here's a typical conversation between me and the Lord:

Clay: "Who, me? Do that? *No way.*"

Jesus: "Yes, you. Do that. *Yes way.*"

That's how a lot of our talks seem to go. I don't think I'm up for some task, and Jesus basically tells me, "Clay, don't underestimate what I can do through you. Now go do it." He's letting me know that He has given me certain skills and abilities to physically do things for others that will help them and glorify Him. Yet so many times I come up with some lame excuse about why I'm not the guy. And again He says, "C'mon, Clay, this task is made for you, man."

Two Men Find Their Passions, Their Callings

I had a friend who could have easily said, "Lord, I'm not the guy. I don't have a college degree. I don't have a lot of money. I don't have some big voice or platform to speak to many people. I'm not the pastor of a church. I'm not on the mission field overseas. C'mon, Lord, I work a very normal job at a tire factory in Memphis, Tennessee. And Jesus, I didn't even come to know You until I was well into my life. What good can I do?"

But my good friend, Hillie Roaten, didn't ever say those kinds of things. Instead, he committed his life to service. And the service he did over and over and over was that of evangelism. That was God's specific calling on his life, and he ran with it.

This guy shared Christ literally everywhere he went. His antennae were always up, looking for an opportunity to tell someone about Jesus. Now get this; Hillie was a layman. *Layman* just means that he was not on staff at a church or employed anywhere in ministry. It's not how he made his living. He was just a normal guy with a normal job. But at the end of his life, this normal guy had led more than two thousand people to Christ. That's right—two *thousand* people! Think about the gravity of that number. Think about the overall effect. Think about the friends and families of those two thousand and how that must have impacted them. And Hillie never preached a sermon. Never sang a solo. Never spoke on TV or the radio. This guy led those folks to Christ *one person at a time!*

Hillie passed away a few years ago. At Hillie's funeral I sang the song "I Bowed on My Knees and Cried Holy." That song paints a wonderful picture of walking into heaven for the first time. I look forward to seeing this hero of mine one day when I'm in heaven. I imagine telling him, "Hey, man, see those two thousand people? God used you to lead them here!"

* * *

Another man who could have said, "Not me, Lord," is Tom Davis. Tom served on staff at several well-respected churches smack in the middle of the Bible belt. Ah, Texas.. "A church on every corner," as they say. As Tom enjoyed secure church work in that fine state, he thrived and was sought after for his skills. But in the middle of his ascent, he started sensing an internal struggle. He was feeling a different kind of tug on his heart. In his book *Fields of the Fatherless*, he related how he felt during that time.

As a pastor, I thought I knew what mattered to God. I read the Bible almost every day. I tithed. I watched the "right" movies. I prayed as often as I could. And can you believe this—I kept my devotions more or less on track and I even journaled in an attempt to reflect on what was happening in my life. But none of this could shake my conviction that there was a big chunk of the gospel I wasn't fulfilling.[xvii]

Tom's eyes were opened on a missions trip to a Russian orphanage. It was there that he felt God's true calling on his life. As he saw the reaction of the children to the service they were getting from his team, he was touched and knew what he had to do.

Tom left his secure, safe position at his church to begin his work at Children's HopeChest, where he serves as president. This missions organization brings God's hope and love to orphans around the world. Their work is focused in the countries of Russia, Romania, and the Ukraine. HopeChest helps churches and corporations around the United States adopt an orphanage and make a real difference in the lives of those kids.

Tom passionately promotes the message that God is deeply interested in three specific groups of people in our world.

"If you searched the Bible from front to back, you'd find many issues close to God's heart.

But you'd also notice three groups of people coming up again and again. They appear so many times, in fact, you have to conclude that God mentions them purposely to make sure they are at the top of our priority list. Allow me to introduce you to those God continually draws our attention to. They are the orphans, widows, and aliens [strangers]." [xviii]

Tom found his place: reaching out to orphans. And he is passionate about it.

Hillie found his place: telling others about Christ. And he was passionate about it.

* * *

I encourage you to ask yourself these questions:

What am I passionate about?

Where is *my place* of service?

What can I do?

How can I serve?

What do I feel burning within me?

How can that passion inside of me break out and impact others?

Let me say it another way. Don't ask yourself. *Ask God.*

These are questions that each Christian man should ask himself. If you haven't before, you can now. Once you figure out the answers, you can start pursuing that thing you know is your calling in life.

Not necessarily your job, but your calling.

That's right; I'm not talking about your job. We looked at that earlier, and it's very important. No, I'm talking about something a little different here. Your calling to Christian service—beyond your job. After all, there are a lot of hours during the week. Hours outside of your workday. For free time, golf, TV, just hanging out with your family. All those things are great, but as Christians we must also be giving some of our time to *serving others*. Billy Graham said, "As Christians we have a responsibility toward the poor, the oppressed, the downtrodden, and the many innocent people around the world who are caught in wars, natural disasters, and situations beyond their control."[xix]

* * *

A Reminder:

Christians are called, in one way or another, to help those in need. Listen, and God will tell you where you can be of service. Remember to ask, *What do You have for me today, Lord?*

The truth is, most guys don't know their passion or calling. They have been busy with other things, like their jobs, and have never really asked God, *Where should I serve?* Or they simply haven't cared enough to find out.

God is asking us, "Do you give a rip? Do you care? Do

you see that there are endless needs and that I have called you to meet some of them?" He is also saying, "C'mon, man, I'll give you everything you need to meet these needs. Don't worry and don't sell yourself short. Just jump in and get ready for an amazing experience!"

As the English preacher John Bunyan wrote back in the seventeenth century, "You have not lived today until you have done something for someone who cannot pay you back." Though I'm not sure this is the way he meant it, it still applies—giving of yourself and your resources to the less fortunate is so powerful, so inspiring, you really *haven't* lived until you've experienced it.

I Want to Do Something, But Where Do I Start?

Dana Key, founder of the early Christian rock band DeGarmo & Key and founding pastor of The Love of Christ Church, Memphis, Tennessee, offered a formula that he suggested to people who wanted to plug in and serve, but didn't know where. It went like this: Passion + Place = POWER. The thinking was that once a Christian determines what his real passion is, the next step is to identify the "where." Once these two factors are added together the result is true power.

This must be committed to prayer. Pray and ask God to show you clearly where He wants you to go and work out this passion that He's put inside you. Once that's determined, watch out! Whoa, Nellie! The real power is coming. Directing your passion will bring powerful results.[xx]

Tom Davis felt this power directly while serving in that orphanage.

> "During my time in Russia, God showed me two life-changing truths. The first was how deeply in love He is with the poor and the outcast. Throughout my stay, I powerfully sensed God loving these kids *directly through me*.
>
> The second truth was how much of God's joy could be mine when I participated with Him in doing something that mattered so much to Him! I had never before experienced God's pleasure and approval as strongly as I did in Russia." [xxi]

Don't you want that power? I do. We all should. I mean, when you think about it, God offers it for all of us. Why do we ignore it? The answer is we just forget or put it out of our minds. I know I do. "Me" and "my desires" and "my time" crowd out the much richer blessing that God is holding for me. I must intentionally ask God to remind me of the true calling on my life and show me how silly my so-called important schedule and agenda can be.

* * *

A Reminder:

Those who serve the less fortunate report that the blessings far outweigh the effort they expend. Want to feel *great?* Get plugged in to a service project!

Maybe you're reading this and still scratching your head about exactly where to get involved in service. You've got to know . . . it's limitless. The needs are everywhere. All around us. And don't just think that the deepest needs are overseas or even across town. I guarantee you that there is a very serious need not far from where you are sitting right now. Maybe a few doors down. Maybe even in the next room. Be a servant. Offer yourself. As Craig Gross and J. R. Mahon of XXXchurch.com wrote in their book *Starving Jesus*,

> "Give to the poor. Feed the hungry. Evangelize on a city street. Help a kid who has cancer. Join the fight against pornography. Share some time with the elderly. Love your neighbor. Play with and teach a little kid. Make yourself available to a teenager who needs a mentor. Fix someone's car. Paint a house. Talk to a homosexual about his or her faith. Pull a drunk out of the gutter, and give him something to eat. Give the homeless guy a place to crash. Bring the hooker to church. Spend the afternoon talking to an inmate at the local jail.   You get the idea. Bottom line: Get off your butt and do something." [xxii]

If you still need direction, I would point you to your home church. Yes, the church you go to. Any church truly focused on Christ will have different service teams doing all kinds of good work. Helping others and glorifying God. If your church does not have any programs that align with your passion, then you should do one of two things: Either start up a new service program there, or leave and find a church that has a program you can get excited about.

This is how our involvement at church should be. Making a difference. Doing something. Impacting our world with the love of Christ. Every church needs to ask, "Are we truly giving the love of Christ to our community? Really? The love of Christ? That's a tall order. Are we doing *that*?" As the popular writer, professor, and preacher Calvin Miller said, "How dare we feel content reading about the works of Christ while a neighbor needs to see a Christ that still works— through people like us."[xxiii] And that's the thing in a nutshell.

Whatever church you go to, if it claims that Jesus Christ is Lord, then it is called to love and reach out to the world. Our churches must be actively touching people in need. Instead of just saying "Let's *go to* church," we need to be saying, "Let's *be* the church!" There's a clear difference.

It's like this: I can *go to* a New York Yankees game. But only twenty-five men can *be* the New York Yankees. Those players don't drive to the stadium thinking, *I'm going to a Yankees game*. No, deep down those guys know, "I am a New York Yankee." Similarly, anyone can *go to* a Tom Hanks movie. But only Tom can *be* Tom Hanks. When it comes to the church, we don't just go—*we are*. We should act like we are the church, and more importantly, we should look and feel that way to the hurting and needy world.

The Church, a Service Organization

In most communities there are many different churches to choose from. This variety has sometimes been called the "buffet line of churches." It's a sad truth that with so many great churches, the public begins comparing the services offered at each one. And just to clarify, I'm not talking about service teams that are reaching the needs of the unchurched and needy; I'm talking about the services offered *to church members.*

I can just hear people browsing for a church, saying, "Oh, this one has amazing music, but that one over there has a wonderful kids program. Then again, the one across town has a brand-new, state-of-the-art family life and fitness center. Before joining a church, we have to evaluate which one will best meet our needs."

Okay, let me just say this . . . I'm all about cool programs for church members to enjoy. I love to watch my children play sports and learn music at church. The men at our church set up a large screen and get together to watch football sometimes. I love the fun activities the youth group does. I love seeing senior-citizen groups going on fun trips to the mountains and such. Book-of-the-month clubs at church. Cookouts. Hayrides. Carnivals. Family festivals. Big, elaborate musical productions at Christmas and Easter. Cooking classes. Art classes.

Each of these activities is great, and they all put a smile on God's face. I mean that. He loves to see His children enjoying themselves with one another. But what clearly does not put a smile on His face is when His children become so self-absorbed that they forget or ignore those outside the church walls who have real needs. He doesn't like to see that we have stopped *serving.*

Erwin McManus, pastor of Mosaic in Los Angeles, stated his concern for how the church is losing its calling to the needy:

> "We were once a church 'on mission' but now
> have become churches that 'support missions.'
> The serving that we are called to requires direct
> contact. You cannot wash the feet of a dirty
> world if you refuse to touch it. There is a sense
> of mystery to this, but it is in serving that the
> church finds her strength. When she ceases to
> serve the world around her, she begins to
> atrophy [the wasting or decreasing in size of any
> part of a body]. When the church refuses to
> serve the world, she begins to waste away. She
> finds herself deteriorating, withering, and losing
> her strength."[xxiv]

Weak and deteriorating? Withering? Losing our
strength? No! God doesn't want us languishing like that. He
wants us to be the strongest men on earth. And we should be!
He wants us to be useful. Useful men who are out there loving
others with our service. With our sweat. With our time. With
our dollars. With our ideas. With our hands. With our
creativity. Not just *talking about* being Christian men. But *being*
Christian men.

James 2:14-17 shouts this loud and clear:

> Dear friends, do you think you'll get anywhere
> in this if you learn all the right words but never
> do anything? Does merely talking about faith
> indicate that a person really has it? For instance,

you come upon an old friend dressed in rags and half-starved and say, "Good morning, friend! Be clothed in Christ! Be filled with the Holy Spirit!" and walk off without providing so much as a coat or a cup of soup—where does that get you? Isn't it obvious that God-talk without God-acts is outrageous nonsense? (MSG)

God couldn't be more clear about this. Talk without action will get you nowhere with God, and as we've discussed, God is the only audience you play to. He wants to see you put your faith into action. Isaiah 58:7-9 also reveals what God wants from us:

What I'm interested in seeing you do is:

sharing your food with the hungry,

inviting the homeless poor into your homes,

putting clothes on the shivering ill-clad,

being available to your own families.

Do this and the lights will turn on,

and your lives will turn around at once.
(MSG)

Lights. God made us to be lights. And by no means does He want us hidden or quiet or inactive. He wants us up there. Out there. Loving His world.

> You're here to be light, bringing out the God-colors in the world. God is not a secret to be kept. We're going public with this, as public as a city on a hill. If I make you light-bearers, you don't think I'm going to hide you under a bucket, do you? I'm putting you on a light stand. Now that I've put you there on a hilltop, on a light stand—shine! Keep open house; be generous with your lives. By opening up to others, you'll prompt people to open up with God, this generous Father in heaven. (Matthew 5:14-16, MSG)

He's pretty relentless—not only about what you should do but also about what the rewards are. Who wouldn't want this?

> If you are generous with the hungry
>
> > and start giving yourselves to the down-and-out,
>
> Your lives will begin to glow in the darkness,
>
> > your shadowed lives will be bathed in sunlight.
>
> I will always show you where to go.
>
> > I'll give you a full life in the emptiest of

places—

firm muscles, strong bones. (Isaiah 58:10-11, MSG)

I like the sound of all that. I really like the part about God showing me where to go. Lord, do I ever need that! And I also like the part about "firm muscles, strong bones." That's what God is offering. Not weakness. Not withering away or deteriorating. He wants us strong, and He is telling us that He will *make* us that way. When? When we reach out to help others in need. When we help and love people who aren't so strong. Folks who possibly never had another person give a rip about them. God will make us strong when we extend a hand to these hurting ones. He's telling us, "Help others, and I will help you."

* * *

Worried About Having to Blaze a Trail? Relax . . . It's Already *Been Blazed*

Stepping into a new area of service can be intimidating. It may involve meeting people on a team who are already doing the work. People you don't know. It may also involve doing work that you are not precisely familiar with yet. Work you've never done before. You might feel a little like the new kid at school, the one who doesn't know anyone. This unsettling feeling keeps most men from stepping into a new area of service. Like me, they think, *I can't do that.* And they argue with God and say, *That missions team is already doing great work. What can I add?*

Trust me here; any service group will be thrilled to have someone new offering their time. In the volunteer world, new blood is always needed. Some wide-eyed person with energy and optimism is *exactly* what most service teams need. Your presence gives them a shot in the arm.

A Reminder:

Service organizations are almost always short on help. You are needed!

Maybe you are thinking about getting involved in something that is brand new. Some idea you can't get out of your head. Something no one at your church or in your community is currently doing. This is where it can really get scary. And all kinds of lame warning signs against following through will pop into your head. You'll be tempted to reason, *Man, if no one else is doing this, maybe there's a good reason for that, and I shouldn't either!*

To that I say, "Don't be a wuss." Be strong. Don't be intimidated. Go do it! Look how Abraham walked into scary and seemingly uncharted territory: "It was by faith that Abraham obeyed when God called him to leave home and go to another land that God would give him as his inheritance. He went *without knowing where he was going*" (Hebrews 11:8). Sounds tough, huh? But the truth is, this was not uncharted territory at all. God knew all about it. God planned it and had been preparing it for His people.

Some might say that even Jesus walked into uncharted territory. After all, He split history in two. He said and did things that no one had ever dreamed. If anyone ever carved out uncharted territory, it has to be Jesus. But that's not the case with His situation either. Where He walked. Where He worked. It had been prepared and worked out before Him. One day some of His disciples were worried about Him and asked if He was hungry. He told them, "The food that keeps me going is that I do the will of the One who sent me, *finishing the work he started*" (John 4:34, MSG).

This work (service) that God is calling you to is on ground He has already been cultivating. It's not uncharted territory. He's been there, and the great thing is, He will be there with you as you serve. God went before Jesus and also went with Him as He served. Likewise, Jesus was before you, and He will also be with you in the service He gives you to perform. In John 14, Jesus said, "The person who trusts me will not only do what I'm doing but even greater things, because I, on my way to the Father, am giving you the same work to do that I've been doing" (verse 12, MSG).

* * *

Invisible Man?

Jesus spoke many times about doing good deeds. Here's His take on the subject:

> "Don't do your good deeds publicly, to be admired by others, for you will lose the reward from your Father in heaven. When you give to someone in need, don't do as the hypocrites do—blowing trumpets in the synagogues and streets to call attention to their acts of charity! I tell you the truth, they have received all the reward they will ever get. But when you give to someone in need, don't let your left hand know what your right hand is doing. Give your gifts in private, and your Father, who sees everything, will reward you." (Matthew 6:1-4)

So much of this is about *motive*. Jesus is not telling us to become the Invisible Man as we serve, so that no one can see or know or even hear about the fact that we are serving. No, Jesus would just rather we not tell others about it ourselves. If folks find out, they find out. We can't really control that. But we don't need to be advertising it. Over and over in scripture, the gift being given seems far less important to God than the heart and motive of the one giving the gift. He's pretty much telling us, "Serve well and serve quietly."

A word of warning here: The more you see being

accomplished by various acts of service, the easier it gets to be prideful. You can even start to think things like *Man, I was the first to show up today. And I did more than anyone else here. But I guess we all will get the same old pat on the back.* Yep, that old competitive drive can rear its head even in Christian service. I've seen it many times. And service teams can say things like "Wow! We have done some great work here. It is amazing what we have done!" Notice the two uses of the word "*we.*" Instead of saying, "Thank *You*, God! Look what *You've* done! Thanks for allowing us to serve!"

Jesus is calling us to serve *humbly*, not proudly. Staying humble is so important in all areas of our lives. And in Christian service it's an absolute must. Whenever I see someone in service who is cocky—whether it be a preacher or a team member—I just can't process that in my mind. Something about it is flat-out wrong. It doesn't fit the job *at all*. I want to tell them, "Man, you need to go into another line of work. Maybe become a talk-show host or a professional wrestler or something." It bugs the fire out of me when I see some arrogant person in ministry. It's just not right. It's off. Don't be that way. Serve humbly.

* * *

A Reminder:

Use Christ as your model for behavior in all walks of life.

Be humble.

If anyone deserves a huge pat on the back for his years of service, it's Billy Graham. After all, this man has led millions to Christ. Millions! If anyone could be excused for saying something like "I've done so much good in my life. God must be so pleased with me," it would be him. But please understand, Billy Graham has *never* said such a thing. It's just not his way. As globally monumental as his ministry is, he has always remained a humble servant. Incredible humility. Much like Christ.

Here's how Billy Graham once described his abilities:

"I am not a great preacher, and I don't claim to be a great preacher. I've heard great preaching many times and wished I was one of those great preachers. I'm an ordinary preacher, just communicating the Gospel the best way I know how. The Lord has always arranged my life so that I have to stay dependent on Him. I just have to stay dependent because I have severe limitations." [xxv]

Now that's remarkable. Billy Graham, a true spiritual hero of our time, basically saying, "I'm not all that. It's God. God is great!" Dr. Graham is focused on Christ, not himself. And that shows in his work. Christ should be our model in everything, including our acts of service. After all, Jesus was unquestionably the greatest, yet He too made Himself a servant.

"But among you it will be different. Those who are the greatest among you should take the lowest rank, and the leader should be like a servant. Who is more important, the one who sits at the table or the one who serves? But not here! For I am among you as one who serves." (Luke 22:26-27)

So Billy Graham said he's not so special. Pretty amazing. And Jesus lowered Himself over and over again. Sleeping in the wilderness. Washing feet. Letting mere men lie about Him and beat Him and (try to) kill Him off. Then He casually reappeared to cook His guys some breakfast before going on up to heaven. Through it all, He remained

175

unthinkably humble.

Yet I look at myself and notice that I have had moments when I got puffed up with pride because I sing little songs and people applaud. How lame of me. I must ask God to continually remind me who I'm serving.

C'mon, Man . . . Have a Heart!

Jesus genuinely cared about the needy. He had deep concern for people's pain. His heart broke when he saw folks who were down and out. He was drawn to them in a magnetic way. And He actually felt their pain.

One day He saw a funeral procession going by. The mother of the dead boy just happened to be a widow. *Bam!* This hit Jesus right between the eyes. (Remember His feelings about widows.) The Bible tells us that when He saw her, "his heart broke" (Luke 7:13, MSG). Notice that it's when Jesus saw the mother, not the dead son, that His heart broke. When He saw her in pain, He felt pain too. He went on to touch the coffin and bring the boy back to life. The Scriptures say that a fearful and powerful celebration erupted. (See Luke 7:11-17.)

On another occasion, Jesus saw Lazarus's friends and family crying over his death. This upset Jesus greatly, and He began crying as well. We might think, *Why did He cry? Didn't He know that in just a few minutes He would raise Lazarus?* Much debate and discussion has taken place over the centuries about exactly what sparked Jesus to weep in this situation. Some say he wept not because Lazarus had died, but because he had to make him come back from heaven to life on earth again. Either way, Jesus knew full well what was about to take place, and he cried with heartfelt sympathy. Compassion filled His heart, and He cried for his friend. He gave a rip. He cared. He sympathized. He felt their pain.

In our acts of service, let's have some compassion. Jesus certainly did. "Jesus made a circuit of all the towns and villages . . . and healed their diseased bodies, healed their bruised and hurt lives. When he looked out over the crowds, his heart broke" (Matthew 9:35-36, MSG).

Am I sympathetic to the needy? Really, am I? Honestly, sometimes I catch myself wondering, *Why can't everyone just be strong and take care of themselves?* I'm ashamed to admit it, but I know I'm not the only one who's had such thoughts. How awful of me to think such things! It's unrealistic and outright selfishness on my part. The fact is, folks who are in need may not have always been in that situation. And many would probably give anything to be able to take care of themselves without help from others. But sometimes they're overwhelmed by circumstances.

* * *

A Reminder:

Instead of looking past the panhandler on the street, think about what may have happened to put him there.

In one of Jesus' parables, He told a story about a guy who, out of nowhere, in an instant, became one of the down and out (see Luke 10:30-37). This guy just got blindsided. Slammed. While walking down a road that, at best, could be described as sketchy and dangerous, he was attacked by thieves. They ripped him off, gave him a serious beatdown, stripped him naked, and left him half dead on the side of the road. Pretty tough day, huh? Lucky for him, a priest walked up. Surely he would lend a hand.

Nope. Nothing. And to make it worse, the priest crossed to the other side of the street, just to distance himself from the poor guy. He didn't want to see him or hear him or smell him. He wanted no part of "that."

After the priest, a Levite happened to walk by. That should have been good news for the poor guy. After all, a Levite would be very familiar with "religious work." It's what he did; he was an assistant to the priests. For sure, he would stop to help.

Nope. Nothing from him either.

Wow, the poor guy lying by the road must have thought, *two religious guys just passed by like they didn't even see me. If they didn't help, no one will. I'm in big trouble. I'm a dead man. That vulture over there is just waiting for me to die so he can get his dinner.*

Then a Samaritan man walked up. The injured man must have thought, *What the??? A* Samaritan? *What does he want? I mean, I've got nothing here. Why is he standing over me?* He probably looked up and said, "Man, what are you doing? You'd better get out of here before someone jumps you too!"

You see, this Samaritan wasn't exactly in his comfort zone; he would have been a very undesirable outcast in that region. As unlikely as it was that a Samaritan would even be there, it was less likely that he would stick around to help the poor guy out. He should have been looking over his shoulder, making sure he wasn't about to get mugged, watching out for himself. But when he saw the injured man, he felt compassion. He hurt for the man, and he offered help. Lifesaving help. And beyond that, after helping the man, he even reached into his pocket to offer future financial help. Amazing.

Jesus called this kind man a "neighbor." In the purest sense of the word, a true neighbor. Not just someone who lives next door, but someone who cares about others whose paths cross his. And Jesus told us, "Go and do likewise" (Luke 10:37, NIV).

As Christian men, we must *not* ignore the great needs around us. Next door. Across town. In the next state. Or on the other side of the planet. Real people with real hurts. Jesus is calling us to step up and serve. And He is telling us that when it's hard and when the needy seem unlovable, as we serve them, we are serving *Him*!

Sometimes I just want to embrace Jesus and thank Him for all He's done for me. The thing is . . . I have found that the only way I can do that is by loving others.

* * *

Don't Forget (A Recap)

Stop saying, *Who, me? Do that?* and start asking God, *Where do You want me to serve?* Then go do it! Be strong. Serve.

Passion + Place = POWER. Determine your passion and

find the right place to live it out. Get ready for powerful results!

Plug in to a church that really *serves*. Or do your part to help make your current church a serving church.

Find comfort in knowing that God has been setting up your work of service. He went before you, and He is now with you in this work. (See John 14:12.)

Serve humbly. It's a must. If not—*and I mean this*—don't bother.

Give a rip. Like Jesus, serve from a heart of compassion. Hurt when others hurt. Then offer help.

Jesus Calls Shotgun

But as for me, the nearness of God is my good; I have made the Lord GOD my refuge, That I may tell of all Your works.

Psalm 73:28

Every word, every sentence, every paragraph, every page, and every chapter of this book has whispered (or shouted at times) this one thought: *Stay close to Jesus.* That's the key reminder in this book of reminders. It is the inspiration behind why I literally placed a little, plastic Jesus figurine on the dashboard of my car. I know . . . it's kind of crazy, but I'm telling you, I need it. I need reminders of Him close to me always. I have discovered that when He's close, I win. But when I allow Him to be crowded out or forgotten, that's when I lose. That's right:

Jesus close = I win.

Jesus not close = I lose.

Every time.

That's why I wrote this book. To remind you to keep Jesus close throughout your whole life. All the time. Everywhere you go. Never forget that He wants to be close to you.

* * *

"Shotgun!"

During my high-school years, whenever I was with a group about to go for a car ride, someone would always shout out, "I call shotgun!" or simply the one word "Shotgun!" It was understood by everyone exactly what that meant. That was how to secure the best seat in the car. You know what riding shotgun is, right? Front seat, passenger side, by the window. The best seat.

Everyone else would scramble for other options. The worst, of course, is the dreaded middle seat. You know . . . on the hump, between people, with no window to look out, all cramped up. Meanwhile the quick-thinking person who called shotgun is up there enjoying the best view, scanning the radio stations, with a cupholder and plenty of legroom.

It's been a long time since I heard someone shout "shotgun," but I have come to realize that Jesus always seems to be calling shotgun with me. That's right. He wants the best seat with me on my whole journey through life. He wants to be right here beside me. He's not that interested in being in the back seat.

Or on the hump.

Or in the car behind me.

Or even in the car in front of me.

Nor does He want to sit home and just wait for my return.

No, Jesus wants to be right here beside me the whole time. Everywhere I go. Whatever I do. With me as I interact with others. And with me when I'm all alone.

Actually, He doesn't want me to be alone. He wants to ride shotgun.

A little disclaimer: I understand that some could disagree with this concept of Jesus wanting to ride shotgun. I can hear them arguing, "Hey, man, I don't want Jesus riding shotgun. I want Him driving the car!"

I totally get that thinking. And, yes, I agree that I want Him ultimately in control. But you know what? I can't get away from the fact that He gives me this little thing called "free will." He gives me the ability to grab the proverbial steering wheel of life and go where I want. He lets me choose. I have options. And while I'm out there making choices and living life, I want Him right there with me (in essence, riding shotgun).

Again, He wants to be close. Check out His words here:

> "Father, *I want those you gave me*
>
> *To be with me, right where I am,*
>
> So they can see my glory, the splendor you gave me,
>
> Having loved me
>
> Long before there ever was a world." (John 17:24, MSG)

Jesus is praying about us! He is expressing His strong desire to be near us. In every situation. Now and for eternity!

Many years before Jesus prayed that prayer, God let Moses know how close He wanted to be to him. Moses was asking God to tell him clearly who would go with him as he led the Israelites into the Promised Land. God told him in no uncertain terms, "*I will personally go with you*, Moses, and I will give you rest—everything will be fine for you" (Exodus 33:14).

God was calling shotgun!

Moses must have liked the sound of that. Then Moses said,

> "If you don't personally go with us, don't make us leave this place. How will anyone

know that you look favorably on me—on me and on your people—if you don't go with us? For your presence among us sets your people and me apart from all other people on the earth."

The LORD replied to Moses, "I will indeed do what you have asked, for I look favorably on you, and I know you by name." (Exodus 33:15-17)

* * *

God had a close relationship with Moses. He even went as far as calling Moses His friend. Talk about living a blessed life!

Here's the thing: We can be that close to God today. Yes, you and I can be just like Moses by insisting that God go with us everywhere. Just like Moses, we should admit that not inviting God along would be disastrous. Just like Moses, we can be friends with God. It's all about saying, *Yes, Lord, please come along. Always. Stay close to me.*

A Reminder:

Jesus wants to "ride shotgun." Make sure He is along for every ride.

I'll Have Mine Rare

Look again at Exodus 33 when Moses asked, "How will anyone know we are set apart from all other people?" In some versions, the word used is *special* or *distinct*.

Special. Distinct. Set apart. Think about those words. That's what God wants from us. As His sons, we are special and distinct. In short, we are different. Set apart from the rest. We are not to talk and act just like everyone else. We are special. In fact, we are very rare individuals. Yes indeed, *rare*.

Jesus knew something about being rare. About not just falling in line and acting like everyone else. He knew a little something about bucking the status quo. He was very comfortable with God's standard, and even when God's standard was not the social norm, He stuck to that standard. And He wants that for us. He wants us to hold true to what He has shown us to be the perfect way. His way.

Toward the end of His Sermon on the Mount, Jesus talked about the way He wants His followers to go. His way. The rare way.

> "You can enter God's Kingdom only through the narrow gate. The highway to hell is broad, and its gate is wide for the many who choose that way. But the gateway to life is very narrow and the road is difficult, and only a few ever find it." (Matthew 7:13-14)

Jesus laid it out there so simply. Ultimately, there are two options for all men.

> *Option 1: His way.* It's not so easy to get through. Not many make it, but some do. And it leads to life.

> *Option 2: The other way.* This one is extremely easy to get through. Many, many people enjoy the ease of going this way. It's effortless. And by the way, it leads to death.

Jesus is whispering, "Hey, man, go with option 1. No, it's not easy, but I'll go with you. I'm calling shotgun. I want to give you life. I don't want to see you die. I don't want to see you give in to the Devil. I don't want your marriage to fail. Go with me and live."

He is calling you to be that rare—special, distinct, set apart—man. That's another important point: Be different! Be set apart! Be that rare man! Commit (or recommit) your life to Jesus. He loves you so much and wants His best for you.

* * *

Having Doubts? You Don't Have To

I wrote this book with fellow Christian men in mind. I assumed that the majority of guys reading it would have already given their lives to Christ. At the same time, though, I have to be realistic and acknowledge that some readers probably don't know Christ. Some will read this book of reminders and think, *I'm not some Christian who needs reminders because, truthfully, I'm not a Christian in the first place. I need Jesus!*

If this is you, if you lie in bed and stare at the ceiling wondering, *If I died tonight, where would I go?* I encourage you to settle this right here and now. I understand that it can be confusing, but hear me when I tell you that Jesus has made the process of coming to know Him very easy. Seriously, He did the hard part (dying on the cross). He has made it easy for us to say, "Yes, *I believe. Please forgive me of my sins and come into my life.*"

If you have never done this, I encourage you to pray the following simple prayer: *Lord, Jesus, I believe You died on the cross for my sins, and I ask You to forgive me of my sins. Please come into my life and be my Lord and Savior. I give it all to You!*

If you prayed that and really meant every word, I celebrate with you. You have been blessed in a way that nothing else can compare to. Because of what Christ did on the cross, you have been forgiven and will spend eternity with Him in heaven.

Right there is why we should rejoice. Right there is why Christians should have this thing called *hope*. Right there is why we should offer these reminders to others. Right there is why we should live lives that say, "Thanks, God!" over and over. Instead of basically saying, "It's okay, God . . . I'm good here."

Again, I rejoice if you just prayed that prayer to receive Jesus into your life. I warn you though—*don't forget*. Don't forget this day. Write down the date and tape it to your mirror or your PC or your dashboard. This is the day that everything changed for you.

You made it through the first go-round, but I challenge you to revisit this little book of reminders. From a different viewpoint. This time read it from the position of a Christian man who wants to *stay* close to God. From the position of a Christian man who wants protection. Not from the position of someone wondering if he is a Christian at all. That's not you anymore. You are in. You are His.

Understand that being a Christian is all about saying,

Lord, I quit. I quit trying to be the boss of my life. I give it all to You. I surrender to Your perfect will and Your perfect love and Your perfect plan for my life!

C. S. Lewis put it this way:

"The Christian way is different: harder, and easier. Christ says, 'Give me All. I don't want so much of your time and so much of your money and so much of your work: I want You. I have not come to torment your natural self, but to kill it. No half-measures are any good. I don't want to cut off a branch here and a branch there. I want to have the whole tree down. I don't want to drill the tooth, or crown it, or stop it, but to have it out. Hand over the whole natural self, all the desires which you think innocent as well as the ones you think wicked—the whole outfit. I will give you a new self instead. In fact, I will give you Myself: my own will shall become yours.'" xxvi

Doing this changes you unlike anything else. I like how Billy Graham described the great change he felt when he came to know Jesus.

"When my decision for Christ was made, I walked slowly down and knelt in prayer. I opened my heart and knew for the first time the sweetness and joy of God, of truly being born again. If some newspaperman had asked me the next day what happened, I couldn't have told him. I didn't know, but I knew in my heart that I was somehow different and changed. That night absolutely changed the direction of my life." [xxvii]

A Reminder:

What do You have for me today, Lord?

Time to Re-Up?

As I've mentioned, in 1998, as a longtime Christian, I rededicated my life to Jesus. A decision which was way, way overdue. That year, I came to a point in my life where I could see clearly just how far away from God I had traveled. I saw just how long it had been since I had taken Him up on His offer to ride shotgun with me. I had left Him behind for years, thinking I was okay. I had followed my own agenda and desires and had lost a close connection with Him. Finally, He broke through to me, and I saw that my only option was to crawl back to Him and ask for His forgiveness.

I'm eternally thankful to tell you that He did indeed forgive me and has walked with me ever since that day. I took Him up on His shotgun offer. And since that time, He has shown me so much. One of the biggest lessons He has taught me is that my life is to be a continual recommitment to Him. I should never feel like I have arrived.

In other words, as I've said before, I am never to take the position, "I'm good here. Thanks, God." Instead, I am always to say, *Lord, I want to be closer to You today than I was yesterday. I rededicate my life to You today!* In essence, that is my daily prayer.

Dear fellow Christian, I encourage you to pray this prayer too. Mean it from your heart, and begin anew today, refocused on Jesus. Pray this prayer of rededication

"Lord Jesus, thank You for saving me. I truly believe I am saved. But, Lord . . . there is currently some distance between You and me, and I want to be closer to You. I have sin in my life, and I ask You to forgive me of these sins [get specific with Him]. Lord, I rededicate my life to You. I want to walk with You in a brand-new way. A closer way. A more real way. And I want others to see that You are everything to me. Give me strength. Give me protection. Give me wisdom. Thank You, Father!

If you prayed that prayer of rededication, I celebrate with you as well! I stand with you. I pray for you, and I challenge you to keep praying it every day.

Let me tell you . . . when I first prayed that prayer in 1998, things started to dramatically change in my life. It's like everything flipped for the better. I began to wonder, *Goodness, was I ever saved or did I just get saved?* I came to realize that I had indeed come to know Jesus as a thirteen-year-old, but that the act of crawling back to Him had great power as well. In fact, I found that all of life has power when it's done close to Jesus. The ups. The downs. The wins. And even the mess-ups and do-overs. When He is with me, I feel His power through it all.

> By his divine power, God has given us everything we need for living a godly life. We have received all of this by coming to know him, the one who called us to himself by means of his marvelous glory and excellence. And because of his glory and excellence, he has given us great and precious promises. These are the promises that enable you to share his divine nature and escape the world's corruption caused by human desires. (2 Peter 1:3-4)

* * *

Don't Forget (One Final Recap)

In this last recap section let's do one final rundown of what we have covered in this book *Dashboard Jesus*. (Just in case we have already forgotten.)

Meet Dashboard Jesus

There's a lot more to your relationship with Jesus than the two main events:

1. *Getting saved.*

2. *Going to heaven.*

Don't get me wrong. Those two events are huge. They mean everything to us as Christians. But, man, there's a lot going on between them. There's your entire life here on earth! And Jesus wants to be close to you the whole way. Through all of it.

Our relationship with God must be more than two dimensional. It's much more than simply asking for salvation, declaring ourselves saved, and then going to heaven at the end of life. We must desire to walk with Jesus every day.

Life is full of distractions, so we have to work at staying focused on God. We need reminders. It's up to us to put them in place.

The Number-One Distraction

We talked a lot about accountability. It's vital to every man with a pulse. Remember those two guys, Brandon and Seth? One of them took the right steps to stay pure, and God protected him from harm. The other guy didn't bother and got slammed.

> Your sex drive is probably the biggest distraction you'll face in your quest to be a man after God's own heart. Get this under control because the potential for disaster is huge.

> The three most powerful reminders you can give yourself are prayer (do it every day), the Bible (read it every day), and an accountability partner (meet regularly).

Uhh . . . I'm Not Much of a Reader

Man, never utter the words "I'm not much of a reader." Start reading the Bible today. Hear me on this one—we've got to have this. It's life. Go to OneYearBibleOnline.com for a printable reading guide.

> Stressed out? Do like Jesus and rely on God's Word for comfort and advice.

> Tempted? Do like Jesus and fire off the Word.

It's not only a history book. It's the *now* book. (See 1 Thessalonians 2:13.)

Jesus was, and is, so serious about God's Word. We should be too.

The Bible is eternally solid. It's perfectly airtight. It is God speaking to you.

So . . . Who'd Like to Say Grace?

Be free and confident in your talks with God. Mix it up a little. Don't bore Him with the same ol' same ol'. He didn't create a robot. He created you. And He wants to hear from you!

Take up fasting, and you will hear from God. Jesus did it and told us to do it. Your stomach might feel empty for a while, but you will be filling up!

Take everything to God. Don't ever assume, "It's okay, God . . . I'm good here." Because truthfully, without Him, we are *never* "good here."

Do a daily detox. Clear your mind. Get quiet with God.

I'm Just a Workin' Man

You spend a lot of your time at work. Make sure you are your real self there, just as you are at home.

Always keep in mind that God is your real boss. Work hard for Him!

Build a solid reputation among your peers at work.

Actually worship God through normal, everyday labor.

When it comes to your view of money, be thankful for the cash . . . but don't be a slave to it.

Who, Me? Do That?

Once you're reading the Bible and praying (asking, *"What do you have for me today?"*), you'll know it's time to get involved on a deeper level.

Stop saying, *Who, me? Do that?* and start asking God, *Where do You want me to serve?* Then go do it!

Remember the equation of powerful service: Passion + Place = POWER. Determine your passion and find the right place to live it out. Get ready for some powerful results!

Serve humbly. It's a must. If not—*and I mean this*—don't

bother serving.

Give a rip. Like Jesus, serve from a heart of compassion. Hurt when others hurt. Then offer help.

Jesus Calls Shotgun

Be that rare man who says, *Jesus, come along with me. Every time. Every place. I want You to ride shotgun!*

* * *

I pray that God uses this book as a reminder for you. The reminders here are certainly ones that *I* must have. Like I've said throughout, guys forget important things. Important truths. Important directions. Important warnings. Important promises. Important offers. Important blessings.

We just forget. This usually comes at the hand of our being distracted. Distracted by our jobs. Distracted by our friends. Distracted by our families. Distracted by ourselves.

I challenge you . . . focus in and stay focused. Do whatever you have to do to keep your mind, your eyes, your ears, and the rest of you focused on Christ. If you live this way, *you will stand out.* You will be different.

And don't worry about being different. Jesus was different. Jesus *is* different. We can be different too. Being different. Being set apart. Being rare. It's a good thing! Thanks for reading.

Here's the book in four words: *Stay close to Jesus.*

Clay Crosse

NOTES

Uhh..I'm Not Much Of A Reader

i Matthew 27:5, NIV.

ii Luke 10:37, NIV.

iii This information is derived from the introduction of *The MacArthur Study Bible* (Nashville: Word, 1997).

iv Read about this in the commentary for Matthew 12:2 in *The MacArthur Study Bible* (Nashville: Word, 1997).

v See Psalm 91:11-12.

vi Read about this in the commentary for Matthew 4:4 in *The MacArthur Study Bible* (Nashville: Word, 1997).

vii John MacArthur, "Introduction to the Bible," *The MacArthur Study Bible* (Nashville: Word Publishing, 1997).

viii This information is taken from a sermon by Pastor Dana Key of TLC Church, Cordova, Tennessee, "Wise in the Word vs. Badly Mistaken," given on November 12, 2006.

So . . . Who'd Like to Say Grace?

ix C. H. Spurgeon, from a sermon "Pleading for Prayer," preached in February 1886.

x Author attended a sermon by Dr. Gary

Chapman at Calvary Baptist Church, Winston-Salem, North Carolina, on February 18, 2007.

xi Craig Gross and J. R. Mahon, *Starving Jesus: Off the Pew, Into the World* (Colorado Springs, CO: Cook, 2007), 104.

xii Jerry Falwell, *Building Dynamic Faith* (Nashville: Thomas Nelson, 2008).

xiii C. S. Lewis, *Mere Christianity* (New York: HarperCollins, 2001), 198.

I'm Just a Workin' Man

xiv Bruce Springsteen, "Factory," from *Darkness on the Edge of Town*, released on Columbia, 1978.

xv Wayne Grudem, *Business for the Glory of God* (Wheaton, IL: Crossway, 2003).

xvi Robert Kahn, *The Ten Commandments for Today* (CITY: Family Library, 1974).

Who, Me? Do That?

xvii Tom Davis, *Fields of the Fatherless* (Prineville, OR: Global Publishing Services, 2002).

xviii Davis.

xix As quoted in *Billy Graham: God's Ambassador* (New York: Time Life Books, 1999).

xx Dana Key, senior pastor, The Love of Christ Church, Cordova, Tennessee.

xxi Tom Davis, *Fields of the Fatherless* (Prineville, OR: Global Publishing Services, 2002).

xxii Craig Gross and J. R. Mahon, *Starving Jesus: Off the Pew, Into the World* (Colorado Springs, CO: Cook, 2007), 18.

xxiii Calvin Miller, *The Words of Christ* (Nashville: B&H, 2001).

xxiv Erwin McManus, *An Unstoppable Force* (Loveland, CO: Group, 2001), 23.

xxv As quoted in *Billy Graham: God's Ambassador* (New York: Time Life Books, 1999).

Jesus Calls Shotgun

xxvi C. S. Lewis, *Mere Christianity* (New York: HarperCollins, 2001), 196–197.

xxvii As quoted in *Billy Graham: God's Ambassador* (New York: Time Life Books, 1999).

Clay Crosse

About the Author

Clay Crosse and his wife, Renee, were married in 1990 and have four children: Shelby, Savannah, Sophie (adopted from China in 2005), and Garrett (adopted from China in 2007).

Clay is a four-time Dove Award winner, including the 1994 New Artist of the Year. He has nine number-one songs, including "I Surrender All," "He Walked a Mile," "I Will Follow Christ," and "Saving the World." Clay continues to maintain an extensive singing, speaking, and worship leading/pastoral schedule.

Clay speaks at men's events, and he and Renee speak at various churches, seminars, and marriage conferences nationwide. Founded by Clay and Renee after they went through a life-changing recommitment to Christ in 1998, HolyHomes Ministries challenges those in Christian homes to be less like the world and more like Christ.

(This ministry is partner supported. To financially support HolyHomes or for booking or other info, visit holyhomes.org. or claycrosse.com. Our mailing address is PO Box 565, Arlington, TN. 38002.)

Other Books by Clay Crosse

I Surrender All: Rebuilding a Marriage Broken by Pornography

Clay and Renee Crosse with Mark Tabb (NavPress, 2005)

Reclaiming Stolen Intimacy

Renee and Clay Crosse (Serendipity by LifeWay, 2008)

———————————————